LIFE IN THE UK

Passing Your Life In The UK Test

Andrew Hannon

LIFE IN THE UK – Passing your Life In The UK test

Easkey Castle Books

Published by Cloontubrid Press

A division of Easkey Castle Books

Copyright © 2015 by Andrew Hannon

First published in the United Kingdom in 2015

ISBN 978-1-326-18791-0

CONTENTS

CHAPTER 1

HOW THIS BOOK WILL HELP YOU

PASS YOUR "LIFE IN THE UK" TEST

This is not a normal textbook...

It's not common for a textbook to begin with an apology, but that is exactly how this one will begin. This book is specifically designed to help you pass your Life In The UK test. As such, the narration of this book is very deliberately crafted towards this goal.

You have already invested your money by buying this book. All that remains is for you to invest some of your time in order for you to get the most out of it that you possibly can. I apologise in advance if at times the book seems to deviate from what you are expecting of it, but try and make a commitment now that you will stick with it to the end. It won't take you a huge amount of time to read it so you have very little to lose. Everything will be clearer by the end.

The ultimate aim of this book...

The ultimate aim of this book is to help you pass your Life In The UK test.

It may also totally transform your approach to learning, but we'll come to that a little later.

So, how will this book help you to pass your Life In The UK test? The answer is, in various ways.

Explaining to you...

The "Why? How? Where?" of the test will be explained but this book will also give you a broader understanding of the test, including some of the criticism it has received. This broader view is not given in any of the official publications, which are too immersed in the subject to be able to take a step back from it. Taking this step back to see the test in a wider context is an essential part in helping you to not be afraid of or intimidated by the test. This book also takes into account some of the less favourable reviews made by readers of the official books, and seeks to address the recurring concerns raised by people who have studied for the test previously.

Relaxing you...

Tests can be stressful, particularly if it has been a while since you have taken one. You might have bad dreams about taking the test or find that you are a bundle of nerves on the day you sit it. This book will help you to realise that there is no need to get stressed when you are prepared.

In the sport of boxing, there is type of punch known as the "snapping punch." It starts with a completely relaxed arm and body and is based on the principle that a relaxed muscle has the greater potential for speed. A similar principle applies to your brain – if it is relaxed before the test, it has a greater potential to perform well.

Amusing you...

It's not likely that this book will be given pride of place in the 'Humour' section of your local bookshop, nor is it likely to be made into a movie with Ricky Gervais. However, it is a far cry from the stuffy, school-text-book type of books which are out there on the Life In The UK test. This does not mean that we do not take the test seriously. Of course we do. It is just that, yes, believe it or not, preparing for your test can in fact be FUN and numerous studies have demonstrated that humour can be a powerful learning tool. Humour, appropriately used, has the potential to illustrate, encourage, reduce anxiety and keep people thinking[1], so there may be a few parts of this book which will hopefully raise a smile from you. If this happens, do not be alarmed!

Assisting you...

The assumption is that you are studying for the exam by using the official *Life in the United Kingdom – A Guide For New Residents* book. This book will not seek to replace your study of the official book, which is an essential part of passing the exam. Rather, it seeks to supplement your studies and increase your chances of passing by showing you some simple but extremely effective learning techniques, tailored specifically to *Life in the United Kingdom – A Guide For New Residents*.

By investing a small amount of time in reading this book, you will soon be able to learn lots of the factual information you will be required to know by using the simple

---

1 IS HUMOR AN APPRECIATED TEACHING TOOL? PERCEPTIONS OF PROFESSORS' TEACHING STYLES AND USE OF HUMOR - Sarah E. Torok, Robert F. McMorris & Wen-Chi Lin

but brilliant techniques described here. You will also learn additional information about some of the people mentioned in the official book which will help you to remember them as *people* rather than just facts. This will all be explained later...

This book will also help you avoid some common errors, which may in the end prove to be the difference between passing the test or not.

Testing you...

At the end of the book you will find ten practice tests based on the learning material from *Life in the United Kingdom – A Guide For New Residents*. These tests are designed to be taken after you have employed the learning techniques and followed the advice from this book.

How this book will work...

You will, of course, find this out as you make your way through the book. For now, it is probably enough to just explain that it will not be replicating everything from *Life in the United Kingdom – A Guide For New Residents*. Rather, this book will mostly focus on a particular section of *Life in* the United Kingdom – A Guide For New Residents and use that section as a way to demonstrate learning techniques that will help you to pass your test. Later on it the book, we will take a look at many of the different people mentioned throughout all of the sections and ways to remember them.

The section this book will be focusing on is **A modern, thriving society** (pages 70 – 117 of Life in the United Kingdom – A Guide For New Residents). This section has been chosen because it is quite varied in what it covers and is therefore the best section to demonstrate how you can employ specific learning techniques to recall lots of separate facts and figures, which is essential for the test.

As with any test, there are no guarantees which questions will come up – it may be that the examples focussed on in this book do come up and you will already know the answers because of the techniques used here. In which case, lucky you! Or it might work out that none of the topics mentioned in this supplementary book come up in the exam... but that's okay. It is worth reiterating that one of the aims of this book is to empower you to use special learning techniques to prepare for questions relating to *any* of the subjects in the learning material. You'll see what I mean as you work your way though the book.

What this book *can't* do...

As helpful as you will find this book to be, it is essential that you are very clear that there is one important thing it CANNOT do, and that is it cannot replace the official book, *Life in the United Kingdom – A Guide For New Residents*, which contains all of the learning material required for the Life in the United Kingdom test. This book that you are holding now is intended to supplement your learning experience and to boost your chances of passing the test, which will mean you avoid having to spend another fifty pounds to take a re-sit of the test, not to mention all of the hassle of having to book it, attend it and go through it all again... I'm sure you have better things to do with your time!

So, if you bought this book thinking that it was the only book you needed to pass your test, I am sorry to disappoint. If you like, you can return it now and get your money back. But if you bought it as a way to bolster your chances of success and to help yourself be as prepared as possible for the test, then sit back, relax and read on...

CHAPTER 2

GETTING TO KNOW

EACH OTHER

A bit of background...

At the moment, in terms of knowing about each other, I have the advantage over you in that I know you are planning on taking your Life In The UK test soon. In case you're overwhelmed by my magical powers, let me explain that that was just a lucky guess.

Although it's not essential that you read this chapter, I'd like to tell you a little bit about me so that you can connect more with the text of this book. The advice and practical tips of this book are presented with good intentions – it is advice which I stand by and in an effort to validate it, I would like to explain a bit about myself and how I came about writing this book to help people who are going to take their Life In The UK test.

I hold dual citizenship, which includes a British passport. As the child of two people who were immigrants to

Britain, I have always (perhaps unsurprisingly) been sensitive to immigration as an issue whenever I hear it discussed.

I having spent the majority of my life in the UK and witnessed a period of huge change. I have fifteen years experience of working for both local and national government and witnessed much change in the way they both function and operate. When I began working for local government, it was considered a 'job for life' – secure and safe and integral to the functioning of the community. These days, rightly or wrongly, we are witnessing large swathes of the public sector being packaged up and sold to private companies, driven by profit and seemingly obsessed with script-reading call-centres.

I mostly enjoyed my time working for different government departments but I feel very fortunate to have got out when I did. I was lucky that one of my hobbies, writing and editing horror fiction anthologies, became successful enough to allow me to do it for a living.

The first time I ever heard of the UK test exams was on the radio, shortly after they had been introduced in 2005. The radio presenter joked that most UK citizens would not be able to pass the exam. I remember thinking "Surely such a test is flawed if people who are from the UK can't pass it... otherwise what good is it?" It reminded me of one of those things you hear about where an ambitious project is ruined by one very small but glaring mistake – an engineer misreads a measurement as inches instead of centimetres, for example, and millions of pounds are wasted before anyone realises the error.

Many years later (and quite recently) I heard mention of the UK Test on the radio once again, with an almost identical observation from the presenter. It could quite literally have been the exact same show from years previously. This time, however, I was not surprised. I had much more experience of working for government departments and therefore had an insight as to how these types of things worked. I had quickly risen up the ranks and was working on project boards, programme boards, cross-departmental programme boards and inter-agency boards. I was working with consultants, Assistant Directors, Directors, Chief Executives, lawyers, Queen's Counsels, Councillors, MPs and members of the House of Lords.

A lot of the people I worked with were very impressive and achieved some remarkable things. However, just as many seemed to be totally clueless.

I recall one department I was working with spending just over a million pounds on consultants to look for ways to save money. The consultants came up with some ideas which could save the department a grand total of... wait for it... half a million pounds. They were quickly escorted from the building.

I was once sent a priority meeting request by a Director to attend a half-day team-building session with several members of the Senior Management Team. The gentleman who ran the session (who charged over one thousand pounds for doing so) taught people to do a full minute of intense pretend-laughing prior to meetings. We also had to shoot invisible snakes. A few weeks later, the same Senior Management Team had to announce budget cuts across the service, which included putting many people at risk of redundancy.

One phrase which kept coming up as a response when some of my colleagues and I raised concerns about the sense of some of the projects which were being commissioned was "We are where we are." This seemed to perfectly sum things up – complain all you want, point out as many absurdities as you like... the fact is, we are where we are and this is what we are going to do. There's a resignation built into the phrase which borders on the beautifully poetic.

Before I digress too much, let me summarise as follows: Government departments can be strange beasts.

Taming the beast...

The test is a requirement under the Nationality, Immigration and Asylum Act 2002. Sounds a little scary, maybe? But it needn't be.

The test has generated much in the way of talk since it was first introduced, and a lot of this talk has been quite critical. Perhaps the most comprehensive and well-observed discussion on the test is Professor Thom Brooks' report *The 'Life in the United Kingdom' Citizenship Test: Is it Unfit for Purpose?*[2] If you are apprehensive about the test, I highly recommend that you read the report, even if you just read the Executive Summary. It's free to read it, it won't take you very long and it will really help you to tame the beast when you see the conclusions that Professor Brooks presents -

---

[2]

http://papers.ssrn.com/sol3/papers.cfm?abstract_id=2280329

unfit for purpose, impractical, inconsistent, trivial and outdated are just some of the highlights.

So why is the test still *the* test?

Remember the words from earlier... we are where we are.

Who's a good citizen?

Yes, we can acknowledge that the test is not actually fit for purpose, but for the time being at least it remains one of the requirements for anyone seeking Indefinite Leave to Remain in the UK or naturalisation as a British citizen. It is meant to prove that the applicant has a sufficient knowledge of British life and sufficient proficiency in the English language.[3]

Here's a question for you to consider. (It's not in the test, by the way.)

---

[3] This definition was taken from Wikipedia, and you may have noticed the inaccuracies here too. 'Britain' does not include Northern Ireland, which is part of the United Kingdom. Furthermore, the test can also be taken in Welsh or Scottish Gaelic, so technically being proficient in English is not required.

You are driving in the middle of the night, lost on a remote country road, and your car suddenly breaks down. Your mobile phone has no signal. A car emerges from the darkness. Would you prefer:

> *a) That the driver of the other car drives past and leaves you (although they do yell out of their window in proficient English that King Richard III was killed in the Battle of Bosworth Field in 1485)?*
>
> *b) That the driver can see you are in need of assistance and stops to help you?*

I know which citizen I would rather happen to be driving the other car. But in fairness to the powers that be who have devised the Life In The UK test, I do not envy them the task of producing a test which could accurately convey whether or not the participant had a sufficient knowledge of British life and whether or not this made them 'citizen material'. It is fairly easy for the newspapers to make fun of the test, but the fact is that devising a perfect test is almost certainly impossible. The parameters used ("sufficient knowledge of British life") are simply too broad and too subjective to really even be termed as parameters, given that British life can be so varied from person to person.

In reality, the test is just a hoop through which one must jump. Do not be intimidated by it, particularly as now you will be more aware of the test in its wider context.

Congratulations – you have taken the first step towards taming the beast.

CHAPTER 3

ABOUT THE TEST

Testing circumstances...

This chapter provides some useful information regarding the Life In The UK test which you will need to be aware of. It will tell you how you can go about booking your test and about the format of the test. Although it isn't the most exciting information, it is worth reading to make sure that you have the necessary things in place to actually sit the test. If you're already aware of it then please skip forward to Chapter 4, which is where the real fun beings...

Why?

The Life in the UK Test is an essential part of any application for citizenship or settlement in the UK. It tests the individual's knowledge of British traditions and customs. It is important to make sure you are fully prepared to book and take the test.

How?

Applicants can sit the test at about 60 test centres across the United Kingdom. Applicants must register with a test centre online or by calling a UK Test Helpline. To register online: https://www.lituktestbooking.co.uk/eass/whatYouNeed.action

To book your test you will need the following:

1. A valid photo ID to check your identity

One of these documents, which has a photo that is a true likeness of you:

- A Biometric Residence Permit, this is a residence permit which holds your biometric information; facial image and fingerprints (must be in date)
- A passport from country of origin (may be out of date)
- A UK photo card driving licence (must be in date)
- A European Union Identity Card (must be in date)
- An Approved Travel Document A Home Office UK travel document: a Convention Travel Document (CTD), a Certificate of Identity Document (CID) or

a Stateless Person Document (SPD) (must be in date)

- An Immigration Status Document, endorsed with a UK Residence Permit with a photo of the holder (may be out of date)

To book your test you must have one of these documents to prove your identity. If you don't have any of these documents, please contact the Home Office.

Please note the name you provide in your test booking must be an exact match to the name contained on the ID you present at the test centre. If your ID includes a middle name, you must include this in the Middle name field or your test will be rejected and you will not receive a refund. If you have registered in your married name and your ID is in your maiden name, you must bring an original UK Marriage certificate, or a UK Spouse Visa (within date), or a UK Deed Poll (this must show a red seal) to support this. Without one of these your test will be refused and you will not get a refund.

2. Valid proof of postcode to verify your address

You must bring proof of your postcode to your test, and this must match the information you entered during registration. From 1st January 2015 candidate proof of postcode cannot be any older than 3 months prior to the date of the Test. We will not let you take your test without this proof, or if it older than 3 months and we will not refund your test fee. This proof should be an original of one of the following documents (photocopies or printouts will not be accepted):

- gas/electricity/water bill
- a council tax bill
- bank or credit card statement (a printed copy of a bank statement is acceptable however it MUST have been stamped and signed by the issuing branch)
- UK photo card driving licence
- or a letter from the Home Office with your name and address on it

You won't be able to take your test without the above documents, so please don't forget to bring them with you.

3. A debit or credit card to pay for your test

The cost of your test is £50.00.

If you do not have a credit or debit card, you can use a pre-paid credit card.

Pre-paid credit cards need to contain the full £50 required to book a test. You can do this by transferring money onto it from your bank account. You can also add money onto your pre-paid credit card at a Post Office and at shops with PayPoint or Payzone facilities.

4.   Your own email address to create your own account

To book a test you need to have your own email address and must register within the system yourself. This is important as all the details regarding your test, will be sent to this email address. Registering for the test yourself is also important as you will be asked to verbally confirm all the details given at registration on the day of your test. You must also present the same method of ID you selected at the point of registration so must be clear as to which method was chosen.

5.   To have read the official Life in the UK handbook

To be ready to take the Life in the UK test, you must have read the official Life in the UK Handbook: A Guide for New

Residents (3rd Edition). When you've read this handbook, you can book your test.

6. To tell the Life In The UK people if you have any special requests

They will do their best to provide the test in a way that meets your needs. They will ask you more about this when you book your test. A special request includes:

- more time to take the test if you've got a visual impairment
- the help of a signer and also more time to take the test if you've got a problem with your hearing
- more time to take the test if you're dyslexic or cannot read in your first language
- the option to take your test in Welsh if the test centre is in Wales
- the option to take your test in Scottish Gaelic if the test centre is in Scotland
- special provision if you only have one legal name and this is displayed on your ID

Booking the test

The test is open to those aged 18 to 65 who wish to become a British citizen. The test costs £50, can be taken at around 60 official test centres in the UK and must be booked at least seven days in advance.

Preparing for the test

To prepare for the test, you should read the book Life in the United Kingdom: A Guide for New Residents, 3rd Edition. You can purchase this online in different formats, such as a downloadable PDF, a book or an audio CD. A study guide and a book of practice tests are also available from the online stores.

There are many resources online that allow you to take practice tests. It is important to understand that these are not the *actual* questions you will be asked, but they can help you to become familiar with the question formats and topics.

What happens at the test?

You'll have 45 minutes to answer 24 questions based on the Life in the United Kingdom handbook.

You must bring the same ID that you used to book the test.

If you don't bring the correct documents you won't be able to sit the test and you won't get a refund.

Test contents

The test covers a range of topics relating to the UK, including:

- The process of becoming a citizen or permanent resident
- The values and principles of the UK
- Traditions and culture from around the UK
- The events and people that have shaped the UK's history
- The government and the law
- Getting involved in your community

Passing

You must get 75% or more in the test to pass. When you do, you will be told straight away and given a Pass Notification Letter by the test supervisor. Make sure you check every detail on it and let the supervisor know if there are any mistakes. You need to keep this letter safe.

You can now proceed with the rest of your settlement/citizenship application. You must send the original with your citizenship or settlement application to prove you passed.

Important - you'll only get one copy of the letter - you can't get a replacement.

Call the Home Office if you've lost your pass letter. You won't get a new one but they'll tell you what to do. Their contact details are Home Office - Lost Pass Letters, telephone: 03001 232 253.

Failing

I'm sure you won't fail if you employ the techniques described later in this book, but if for some reason you don't pass, you must wait 7 days before taking the test again. You can take the test as many times as you need to but you'll need to book and pay again each time.

CHAPTER 4

AN INTRODUCTION TO

A LEARNING TECHNIQUE

Big deal for King Richard III

So we've done the bit where I explain what this book will do for you. We've done the introductions. We've covered how you can book your test and what you can expect on the day of it. One more chapter before it's time for some learning.

As mentioned previously, we are going to mostly focus on a particular section of the official *Life in the United Kingdom – A Guide For New Residents* book, *A Modern, Thriving Society*. It makes sense to do this because you will be able to study this particular part of the learning material at the same time as I introduce you to mnemonics.

Earlier on in the book, I mentioned a scenario where a driver of a car doesn't stop to help you when your car has broken down, but he does yell out of his window at you the year that King Richard III was killed at the Battle of Bosworth Field.

Can you remember the date?

I'm going to guess that you probably can't.

Now what if I asked you what your own date of birth is? Of course, you'd have no trouble recalling it. How about your boyfriend's/girlfriend's birthday? Again, the chances are that'd be no trouble for you.

So what's the difference?

That's probably pretty obvious. Your date of birth and the birthday of your partner actually mean something important to you. Your brain has committed them to your long-term memory because they are important and significant to you. Let's face it, knowing that King Richard III was killed in the Battle of Bosworth Field in 1485 isn't likely to have the same level of emotional significance for you – you certainly didn't know the man personally.

King Richard III's death is unlikely to ever be very useful to you beyond the purpose of it being a question in the exam (unless you go to a lot of pub quizzes). The cold, hard, brutal fact here is that no-one cares when he died. It simply doesn't matter anymore. The case is closed. His death is only important if it comes up as a question in the exam.

This is an extreme example... I don't want to make light of Richard's death but his grim demise helps to illustrate a point. Even something which seems like quite a "Big Deal" (in this case, the death of a King of England on a bloodied battlefield) can be difficult to remember if there is nothing to anchor it firmly into your memory. Along with all the other facts you will try to memorise for the exam, it is in danger of being swept away beyond the point of recall.

For your date of birth or the birthday of your boyfriend/girlfriend, you'd be able to respond correctly almost without thinking because the date means something to you beyond an exercise of factual recall, unlike King Richard III's death. The brain is particular about where it stores information and it is unlikely to store the date of King Richard III's death in the same compartment it uses for meaningful dates.

And that is the point here. You need to bear in mind that you are studying to pass an exam. As soon as the exam is over, it's okay to forget when King Richard III died.

Therefore, we need to employ a different technique to help us recall when King Richard III was killed. A technique which will allow you to store it quite securely in your short-term memory for the purpose of passing your Life In The UK test.

Mnemonics

It's not the most attractive word but it may just change your approach to learning...

To hear how the word is pronounced, touch the word on your screen (if you are reading this on an e-reader) or scratch the word if you are holding the print edition, then say 'Voice activation initiated.'

Okay, that was a joke. Maybe not very funny but I want to try and put you in the right frame of mind when it comes to approaching and using mnemonics – have fun with it and you will be amazed and astounded at how much it can help you to achieve.

History lesson

Quite simply, a mnemonic is any learning technique that aids you in information retention. The chances are you already know of a few. Perhaps you used a rhyme to help you learn how to tie your shoelaces when you were little. Or maybe you used one to help you learn your left hand side from your right hand side.

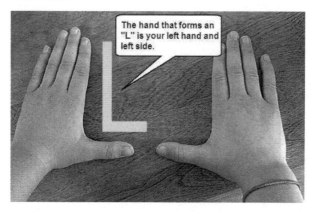

Ancient Greeks and Romans distinguished between two types of memory: the "natural" memory and the "artificial" memory. The former is inborn, and is the one that everyone uses automatically and without thinking. The artificial memory in contrast has to be trained and developed through the learning and practicing of a variety of mnemonic techniques.

Mnemonic systems are special techniques or strategies consciously used to improve memory. They help employ information already stored in long-term memory to make memorisation an easier task.

"Memory Needs Every Method Of Nurturing Its Capacity" is a mnemonic for how to spell mnemonic.

Lots of the early exponents of mnemonics were thought to be sorcerers because people could not accept that memory could be so good! In reality, it's just using the brain in a creative way to help trigger memory.

My experience with mnemonics

I first learned about mnemonics in 2007 when I was studying for some qualifications specific to my job at the time. It was a year long course which entailed a full day at college every fortnight, which didn't sound too bad when I signed up for it... I got to leave the office and meet some nice people from around the country who were also studying for the qualifications.

However, the studies soon resulted in the total loss of every weekend as I was tasked with writing essays and reports and having to familiarise myself with subjects I had no previous experience of in order to pass all four modules.

It was a lot of learning and I approached it the only way I knew how – lots and lots of repetitive reading, hoping that the facts and figures would eventually sink in and stick.

About a month before the exams, the course organisers arranged for a study week at a university in the north of England. We went from one super-intense revision class to another. It was intense.

At the end of one particularly tough and arduous class, a fellow student approached me and said that the only thing that had kept him awake during the class was watching me as I constantly battled to keep my eyes open and prevent my head from hitting the desk. The revision was not going well...

The next day, I attended a class which, at the time, I thought was even worse. A very, very enthusiastic teacher sang the praises of what he called 'mind maps' – using visual images to help you remember a large number of facts. I remember thinking that it sounded even more complicated than the things I was trying to learn and I was very resistant to the idea. I took the handouts from the class but it was only a couple of weeks later, in the depths of desperation and in the realisation that the usual method of just constant reading was not going to do the trick, that I thought I would give the technique a try for a couple of hours, just in case it helped...

And I never looked back.

By the end of two weeks, I was able to recall a huge amount of facts, figures, dates, regulations, and laws... everything I needed to know. I was *astounded* by the results – little wonder that people would be thought of as sorcerers back when mnemonics started! It worked so well for me that I genuinely felt as though I had developed superpowers! I could recall a huge amount of information that had previously been evading me just by calming thinking. I sat the exams and passed all four modules. I know for a fact I would not have been able to if I hadn't used mnemonics.

I'm really conscious of how much resistance I originally felt towards mnemonics as a technique, so if you're thinking the same now then I know exactly how you are feeling. But as you have invested in this book, you owe it to yourself to give it a try. Like I did, just initially give it a couple of hours and see how you feel then. What have you got to lose?

CHAPTER 5

A MODERN, THRIVING SOCIETY

PACKED NEATLY INTO YOUR BRAIN

Applying the principles to what you need to know

We are going to focus on *A modern, thriving society*, which form pages 70 to 117 of the *Life in the United Kingdom – A Guide For New Residents* book. We will go through it section by section and use mnemonic techniques to help you easily memorise the information presented.

As we go further through, you are encouraged to use your own mnemonic techniques, as the experience will help you when you take the same approach to studying the other chapters in *Life in the United Kingdom – A Guide For New Residents*. (The other chapters are *The values and principles of the UK, What is the UK?, A long and illustrious history* and *The UK government, the law and your role.*)

A modern, thriving society is the section which tells you about aspects of life in the UK today. It is split into the following categories:

- The UK today
- Religion
- Customs and traditions
- Sport
- Arts and culture
- Leisure
- Places of interest

If you haven't already done so, let's start off with you reading *A modern, thriving society* all the way through. When you have finished, take a look at the ten questions which follow and get a general feel for how much of the information you remembered.

Mini Test 1 – 10 Questions

1. When is Boxing Day?

- ○ The day after Christmas Day
- ○ The day before Christmas Day
- ○ 31 December
- ○ 1 January

2. Who is a Scottish Cyclist who has won six Gold Olympic medals?

- ○ Sir Chris Hoy
- ○ Sir Ian Botham
- ○ Dame Ellen MacArthur
- ○ David Weir

3. When is Valentine's Day?

- ○ 15 February
- ○ 14 February
- ○ 16 February
- ○ 12 February

4. The main Olympic site for the 2012 Olympic games was in

- ○ Oxford Street, West London
- ○ Stratford, East London
- ○ Millenium Stadium in Cardiff
- ○ Wembley Stadium in London

6. Which two are Protestant Christian groups in the UK?

- [ ] Buddhists
- [ ] Roman Catholics
- [ ] Methodists
- [ ] Baptists

7. Who won the men's singles in the US open in 2012?

- [ ] David Weir
- [ ] Andy Murray
- [ ] Jessica Ennis
- [ ] Ellie Simmonds

8. Diwali normally falls in

- [ ] October or November
- [ ] January or Februaury
- [ ] August or September
- [ ] June or July

9. When is St Patrick's Day?

- [ ] 17 March
- [ ] 1 March
- [ ] 23 April

Special days, sports, religions, places of interest... It's a wide area of study and it might be difficult for you to differentiate your April Fool's pranks from your Halloween trick or treats, or your Ian Bothams from your Andy Murrays if you're not particularly into cricket or tennis.

The answers are at the back of the book if you want to check later, but perhaps you already have a feel for how well you did based on how many you actually knew and how many you had to take a guess at. In any case, we will revisit these questions in a little while so don't worry about checking the answers right now.

Using mnemonics, we're going to go through *A modern, thriving society* together and look at ways of memorising lots of the information so that we can recall it quickly, accurately and easily.

The UK today

We'll ease into things here and start with this question.

What is the distance (in miles) between the North coast of Scotland and the South coast of England?

○ 270 miles

○ 470 miles

○ 870 miles

○ 1070 miles

If you're like me, your understanding of a mile is probably restricted to low figures in most of your everyday life. For example, it's five miles to my nearest supermarket, or I try to go for a ten mile run every Sunday. Beyond that, I'd find it hard to gage and appreciate the distinction between three hundred miles or four hundred miles – they both seem pretty long to me.

For the answer to the above, you could just keep reading the answer again and again and again until eventually you thought "Okay, I've got it. From the North coast of Scotland to the South coast of England is 870 miles." Which is fine... but then the question might not come up, so you have used a very focussed and intense part of your short-term memory for nothing.

An alternative way to remember it is to imagine a scenario based on the question and its answer in the form of something visual and interactive. We can also incorporate other visual elements into our scenario to help us recall other facts from the *A modern, thriving society* section in a really simple way.

We know it's a fairly long way from the top of Scotland to the bottom of England. That's a given, and that's why we have trains and motorways which allow us to travel at high speeds between one and the other. So let's imagine a train station at each end. You're at one of the train stations - let's say Scotland for this example – and you know that your train to the South of England leaves at 8.00am. You're nice and early so you have time for breakfast before your train leaves, and you decide to have a big breakfast because you are going to skip lunch and have a big dinner when you get to the South.

While we're talking about food and countries, it mentions in *Life in the United Kingdom – A Guide For New Residents* that a traditional Scottish food is haggis. So let's say you have haggis for breakfast and, when you get to the South of England, you're going to have the traditional English meal of roast beef. (This is an imaginary exercise, so if you're a vegetarian you can either play along or simply have vegetarian haggis and vegetarian roast beef.)

We can see that as a visual in the following map:

There's the haggis (or vegetarian haggis) up in the North of Scotland, and there's the roast beef waiting for you down in the South of England.

So, top and bottom, breakfast and dinner, trains... how does it all link to helping us remember the answer to the question?

I've been on hundreds of trains and they move pretty fast (when they move). But I couldn't tell you if they moved at 80 miles per hour or 120 miles per hour. Let's just say they move at 100 miles per hour – a nice and easy number to remember, and probably about right.

We've had breakfast just before 8.00am and we're getting a train to the South of England in time for dinner...

What is the distance (in miles) between the North coast of Scotland and the South coast of England?

○ 270 miles

○ 470 miles

○ 870 miles

○ 1070 miles

Well if it was either of the first two answers, we would be far too early for our dinner. We'd arrive at about 10.40am and

12.40pm respectively, and we'd still be full from the big haggis.

If it was 1070 miles and the train was doing 100 miles per hour, that would take over ten hours and we wouldn't get to the South of England until about 6.40pm. We've skipped lunch too so we would be very, very hungry.

But if the answer is 870 miles, we'd arrive for dinner at just before 5.00pm. Perfect for an early dinner after a long train journey without lunch!

I know, I know, at first this might sound very confusing... maybe even far more difficult than just reading and reading the learning material over and over again... But take a second and think about the story. As absurd as it might be, there is a structure and a *sense* to it. It uses concepts and ideas that you understand – breakfast time, the speed of a train, dinner time. It also helps you to associate certain foods with certain places in the United Kingdom. Seeing a giant haggis at one end of a map and a huge plate of roast beef at the other will stick in your mind for a lot longer than words on a page will.

Using the story, you'll realise that the first two answers are too short, and the last one is too long, especially as you skipped lunch! You can even forget the answer is 870 miles and still be able to figure it out from the options using the story, plus you have the answer to other potential questions too! You might also decide to amend the story and make it your own. For example, your train might go through Wales briefly and you decide to have a small lunch of traditional Welsh cakes. Or a passenger who boards the train in Scotland introduces himself to you as Andrew, another passenger gets on in Wales and introduces himself as David... and you're learning the names of the patron saints. The sky is the limit!

This is the type of technique you can apply to lots of the other facts and figures in *Life in the United Kingdom – A Guide For New Residents*.

Religion

Religions are quite varied in the UK. Depending on what country you yourself come from, you may or may not have experience of these different religions.

If you're not familiar with Christianity, the two big important things to remember are Easter and Christmas. Christmas comes up a lot in the *A modern, thriving society* section of the book in terms of traditions followed and significant dates. If you've been in the UK over a December period, the chances are you would have noticed Christmas, as most Christmas adverts start on TV in about early November and spend the next eight weeks trying to persuade you to buy things at *amaaaaaazing* prices... then as soon as Christmas is over, the adverts tell you about the sales, where you can get things at *amaaaaaazing* prices... You catch my cynical drift.

Anyway, rather than drawing maps for Christmas, this is just an area of the book where it is worth learning it by rote. It's fairly straightforward and you won't have any problem with it. It boils down to: Christmas is on 25 December (therefore Christmas Eve is 24). Boxing Day is the day after (imagine loads of empty boxes which had previously contained presents at *amaaaaaazing* prices). And people traditionally eat turkey.

Based on the test questions I have researched, that's essentially Christmas covered!

Easter is easy too, although maybe one or two of the names associated with it will be difficult if you're not familiar with the Christian calendar. Here are a couple of questions to look at:

The 40 days before Easter are known as _____

○ Easter holiday

○ Lent

○ Santaday

○ Winter holiday

The answer is Lent. But how can you recall that easily?

There's a kind of structure to it which will help you remember. Lent itself is not a festival – it's a period of forty days which leads up to the festival of Easter and it is traditional for Christians to give something up for that forty day period. For example, someone fond of chocolate might decide to not eat chocolate for that period.

And that's where Shrove Tuesday comes in. It is the last day before Lent so people go a little over the top. That's why people have pancakes... because they're naughty but nice and represent all the things they are going to have to make do without for forty days. They use them all up because they won't be able to have them for forty days.

It's handy that 'Lent' is spelt the same as 'lent', because it helps with the next question.

Lent begins on _____
- Good Friday
- Ash Wednesday
- Good Friday
- St Valentine's Day

Imagine you have a friend called Ash and you lent him (or her) a five pound note on Wednesday. The image of you giving something up (in this case, a five pound note) will help you recall that Lent is a period where people 'give things up', and the image of a person called Ash should be enough to associate Ash Wednesday with the beginning of Lent. By default then, you'll know that the day before must have been Shrove Tuesday when people were going crazy over pancakes covered in syrup and sugar.

To really help you remember, it's worth repeating – the massive clue is in the word 'Lent'.

At the end of Lent, it's Easter. The symbol for Easter? What's one of the ingredients for pancakes? That's right – an egg. So we've come full circle.

This is a fairly basic overview but ought to be sufficient based on the test questions for the Christian festivals.

One question which seems to pop up a bit in one form or another and is worth touching on is :

What is the Church of England formally known as?

⚪ The Methodist Church

⚪ The Anglican Church

⚪ The Baptist Church

If you don't already know the answer then I'd like you to look at the options and take a guess. Have a think about it for a moment or two and try to make it a guess based on something that you might notice.

The answer is 'The Anglican Church' and the reason I wanted you to guess if you didn't already know this is because of the similarities between En**gl**and and A**ngl**ican. They even share the Engl**and** and Anglic**an**. If you've ever studied French then you will know that the French for England is Angletere. That's all Anglican means – English.

Here's the question again, worded slightly differently:

The Church of England is also called

○ Scottish Church
○ Welsh Church
○ Anglican Church

Knowing that Diwali means 'festival of lights' provides a clue as to when it is in the year.

Diwali normally falls in

- ◯ October or November
- ◯ January or Februaury
- ◯ August or September
- ◯ June or July

Out of all of the months presented above, when would you most likely be in need of a light? I would associate October and November as being the darkest months – the clocks have gone back, the sun sets so early... that's when I would need a light the most.

Here's a handy hint for remembering the answer to this question on Vaisakhi (Baisakhi).

Vaisakhi (also spelled Baisakhi) is celebrated on _____ each year with parades, dancing and singing

- ◯ 14 January
- ◯ 14 April
- ◯ 14 July
- ◯ 14 October

It's unusual for there to be two different spellings, so let that be the thing you remember – your anchor. Anchors are important in mnemonics – they help keep our facts stored in one place and we can retrieve them from the depths whenever we need to!

So, the V and the B are interesting... it means the first consistent letter is 'A', which is our anchor for the month of April, which is the correct answer.

"Ah ha!" You might say. "But what if I get confused and think of August?"

That's a good point, so let's look at the question again and see if there is anything which might help us more... parades... dancing... singing... That's the one! Singing! If we think of the famous Gene Kelly song *Singin' In The Rain* then we can associate that with 'April showers', when the rainfall in the UK is at its highest. It doesn't rain so much in August, so we know that out of the two months beginning with the letter 'A', Vaisakhi (Baisakhi) is celebrated in April.

Once again, I appreciate that this might all seem confusing at first and you might think it's a crazy way to remember things... But if you see that question in a similar form any time in the next few days, you'll automatically think "I remember the name of that festival. It's the one with the two different spellings. Why is that significant...?" And so your thinking will progress and you *will* remember April.

You'll realise exactly how powerful this technique is when you come to the test questions at the end of this book.

Customs and traditions

On the test practice questions, you'll notice a lot of questions on saints and their days. Here's a nice visual way to remember all of the four UK countries' saints and which dates they fall on.

First of all, let's visualise a map of the UK.

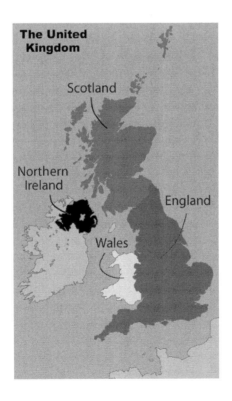

Northern Ireland's patron saint is St Patrick, Wales' patron saint is St David, Scotland's patron saint is St Andrew and England's patron saint is St George.

They are all fairly common names in the UK, so the chances are you know a few people with some, if not all, of the names. But even if you don't know any one by those names personally, I'm sure you can think of at least one famous person with each of the names. For example:

Patrick Stewart, who played Captain Jean-Luc Picard in the *Star Trek: The Next Generation* series.

David Cameron, the Prime Minister (at the time of writing).

Andrew Dufresne, from one of the greatest movies of all time, The Shawshank Redemption

George Clooney, the most suave man in Hollywood.

If you don't know any of them then think of your own examples of people with the same first names. They don't need to be famous.

Okay, next thing we're going to do is to put them on the map, into their respective saints' countries.

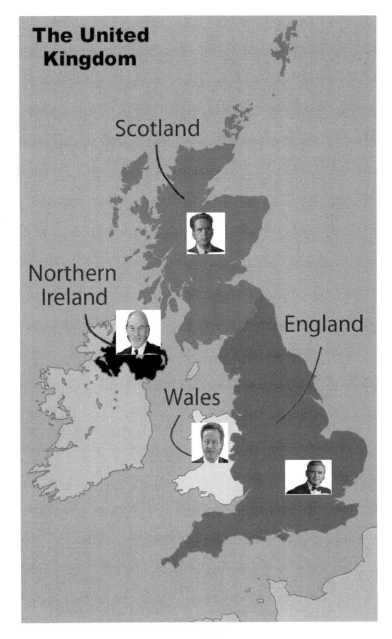

Next we need to get some action and interaction going between the four of them. This is where it might start to sound silly, but as I will say throughout this book, stick with it.

St Patrick's Day is on 17 March and St David's Day is on 1 March. So let's imagine both Patrick and David *march*ing on the spot. They're both lifting their left leg and then their right leg, marching away, left, right, left, right. As Patrick is both older and higher up than David, that's two visual clues that out of the numbers 17 and 1 (for 17 March and 1 March), Patrick is more associable with the higher number.

Now let's imagine that David is marching in a puddle. He is marching so hard that he is splashing up lots of water, and the water is raining down on George in England. George doesn't want to get wet, so he puts up an umbrella. In England, as mentioned earlier, there is a term called 'April showers' because it seems to rain so much in that month. So we now have a link for George and England and April.

And what about Andrew, all the way up in the top of the picture? He's so far away having escaped from

Shawshank prison that there is NO easy Way to rEMBER him... NOWEMBER.

Not perfect, but work with it!

So based on all of that seeming nonsense, the map now looks like this:

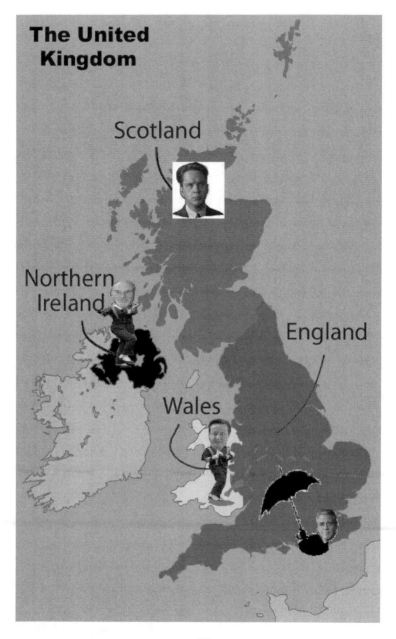

There's **Patrick**, older and higher up than David, **march**ing away.

There's **David** too, **march**ing away, splashing water onto George.

George takes his umbrella out to protect himself from the **April** showers.

And no change for **Andrew** up in Scotland, for whom we have **NO W**ay to r**EMEMBER.**

I know it sounds silly, maybe even childish. But who cares? You *will* remember it far more easily than you would remember a list of names and dates.

Who is David splashing water on? Who's the older and higher marcher? If you had no way to remember the month of November, wouldn't the fact that you had 'no way' *remind* you that it was November? Which celebrity has an umbrella and what month in particular would an umbrella be useful to keep handy?

This will stay in your memory because there is a story behind it, albeit a very strange one.

Grab a pen and paper now and do a quick sketch of the map, from memory, with all four of the people on it and a few words describing what they are doing and their relationships. If you get stuck, just think about one particular thing and see if it unblocks your mind. I bet your sketch will be finished quickly and it will be 100% accurate, or close enough to it, so that you can use it to know which country has which patron saint and the months in which the saints' days are celebrated. Then use your sketch to help you answer the following questions.

Who is the patron saint of Wales and on which date is his feast day?

◉ St Michel 3rd March

◉ St Peter November 29th

◉ St James 5th September

◉ St David 1st March

What is the correct order of the National Days?

◉ St George's Day, St David's Day, St Patrick's Day, St Andrew's Day

◉ St David's Day, St Patrick's Day, St George's Day, St Andrew's Day

◉ St Patrick's Day, St David's Day, St Andrew's Day, St George's Day

◉ St David's Day, St Patrick's Day, St Andrew's Day, St George's Day

What is the name and the date of the National Day of Wales?

○ St Andrew's Day, 30 November

○ St Francis's Day, 19 June

○ St George's Day, 23 April

○ St David's Day, 1 March

St Andrew is the Patron Saint of _____

○ Scotland

○ Wales

○ England

○ Northern Ireland

Easy! I bet you got all of them right.

Sport

Not everyone likes sport, so listing a load of sportspeople's names and expecting you to be excited by them is another example of where the idea behind the test is... well, a bit silly. I'd be much happier having a chat with someone about Spanish football than I would be discussing cricket. I don't understand cricket, nor do I want to, and if I was Prime Minister, the first thing I would do would be to ban it and build a football stadium on ever cricket pitch in the country. No more hearing about England versus Australia in the Ashes tournament every two years!

As for the London 2012 Olympic Games, quite a lot of Londoners were initially quite resentful towards hosting it because part of the costs were added to their council tax bills while the rest of the country didn't have to pay a penny. And let's be honest... when would many of us otherwise be interested in athletics? The answer is 'Never'.

In today's celebrity obsessed world, after the Games ended, lots of the athletes were suddenly famous and their names were known in every household. So what happened? What do we do with famous people when what they are famous for only takes place once every four years? Well, they all took it in turns to appear on a load of comedy panel shows and celebrity versions of TV quiz shows until finally most of them were forgotten.

Anyway, let's look at ways of remembering some of the sports people listed in *A modern, thriving society*. We are going to look at ten of the people referred to as 'Notable British Sportsmen and Women' and learn just enough about them to help you get some more anchors. No matter how tenuous or silly some of these examples sound, they *will* stay in your memory.

Sir Roger Bannister

Sir Roger Bannister ran a mile in under four minutes in 1954. If only everyone had such a visually rich surname, mnemonics would be even easier! The obvious thing to focus on here is the speed at which Sir Roger ran. And what's another way to go fast? To slide down a banister would be a good way!

Sir Jackie Stewart

A fantastic Formula 1 driver. Think of a car-jack (Jackie) for when you need to change a tyre on a car. If that's not enough, imagine you are eating stew. What might cause you spill it over your lovely white trousers, creating a new form of art? Stew-art. Being driven around a race track really fast might cause it.

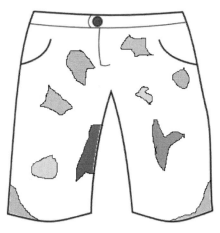

Yes, absurd... but when you get two words which form a surname like 'Stew-Art' then it's a gift for memorising. And your mind will easily (and logically) connect the 'stew art' to 'What caused the stew to spill onto the trousers?' It would be more likely that it was from being driven around in a fast car than, say, playing football.

Sir Bobby Moore

Captained England's football team in 1966 when they won the World Cup. Look at the name 'Bobby'... what do the two lower-case 'b's look like?

B O 6 6 Y

Sir Ian Botham

One of England's best cricketers. His nickname is Beefy, owing to his physique. Ian 'Beefy' Botham. If you can remember that then you can imagine a cow in a field playing cricket.

Sir Steve Redgrave

An awesome rower. His surname is our anchor. Visualise a red gravestone (Redgrave) with two oars. I know it doesn't make any sense, but you will remember it if his surname comes up in the test!

Sir Chris Hoy

Sir Chris Hoy is a cyclist. The anchor here is the 'Sir Chris', which sounds a bit like 'circus'... so let's imagine a circus clown cycling on a bike.

Bradley Wiggins

A cyclist and the first Briton to win the Tour de France. His surname is unusual so that's our anchor. Imagine a man cycling on his bike so fast that his wig (Wiggins) flies off.

Andy Murray

There's no denying his tennis skills, but what *Life in the United Kingdom – A Guide For New Residents* fails to mention is that Andy Murray has possibly the most boring voice in the world. Look up any interview with him on YouTube and you'll see. I'm sure he's a very nice guy but in order to help you remember who he is, just focus on his name. Andy... Murray... Andy... Murray... It kind of rhymes and has a similar back-and-forth quality to it that you would get in a never ending tennis rally... back and forth, back and forth, Andy, Murray, Andy, Murray... hypnotic... repetitive... dull. So if you're sitting in the test and a question comes up with the name 'Andy Murray' in it, focus on your anchor, the little chant 'Andy... Murray... Andy... Murray...' and it will unlock your knowledge that he is a very boring (but very good) tennis player. The clue is in the name – we don't even need a visual for this.

Mo Farah

Another sportsperson we don't need a visual for. Mo Farah is a phenomenal distance runner (I once raced with him, but I was about eight thousand places behind him so I doubt he'd remember me). Again, look at his name. *Far*ah. Far. He runs *far*.

David Weir

A *six time* marathon winning wheelchair athlete who goes by the nickname 'The Weir-Wolf' (as in werewolf). So imagine a wolf speeding along underneath the full moon in a wheelchair and you'll remember David Weir.

That's ten examples of how you can memorise names and associate facts with them visually. If you took even five minutes to memorise those pictures and the descriptions, you would be able to recall all of them for a long time afterwards. It's all about the anchors, so when you make your own make them as personal and as obvious to you as you can and that will make them even easier to recall. You will find that your brain automatically groups all of them together – you will see that it is a sport question from the question itself, your brain will start to fire up all the images of giant sixes which look like the letter 'b' and red gravestones with oars, and then you know that somewhere in the name your anchor is embedded.

In Chapter 6 of this book, we will do something similar for ten different people mentioned in the learning material, but for now we will carry on with the rest of *A modern, thriving society.*

Arts and culture

A modern, thriving society lists seven composers and gives you information on them, such as which pieces of music they wrote. If you like classical music then you are probably fine for this part, but if you don't know much about it then it can be difficult to make the connections, particularly as seven different composers is quite a lot.

Let's take a look at them:

Henry Purcell

George Frederick Handel

Gustav Holst

Sir Edward Elgar

Ralph Vaughan Williams

Sir William Walton

Benjamin Britten

Do you notice anything immediately memorable about any of the names in comparison to each other? Take a look again...

Henry Purcell

George Frederick Handel

Gustav Holst

Sir **E**dward **E**lgar

Ralph Vaughan Williams

Sir **W**illiam **W**alton

Benjamin **B**ritten

It might not appear much, but it's a start – three of the seven composers – almost half of them - have first names and surnames which begin with the same letter. Something else is that of those names, the letters 'E', 'W' and 'B' are an anagram of the word 'web' so we could imagine three composers on a giant spider web.

The image is unusual but you will be able to retain it. Think about what it is telling you. Composers and web. Web. What is the link? As so often, it's the names. So if you get a question asking you if Sir Edward Elgar was a composer or a carpenter, take a second and see if the 'E E' name triggers your memory. You may find that the image above is just enough to make sure you select the correct answer.

Other little techniques for memorising information about the individual composers are as follows.

Henry Purcell

As stated in *A modern, thriving society*, Purcell played the organ at Westminster Abbey. To link the name Purcell with an organ, let's think of the famous cleaning product Persil, which is pronounced very similarly. Then imagine a big, shiny, clean organ, gleaming away.

The thought process here is the connection between 'clean' and the organ, which is how Purcell/Persil becomes the anchor. It should be enough for you to associate Purcell with playing the organ rather than any of the other composers, even if Persil would be an unlikely cleaning product to use on a pipe organ!

George Frederick Handel

One of the facts about George Frederick Handel is that he was born in Germany and later became a British citizen. Once again, we have a massive clue in the name:

Ge**or**ge Frederick **(m)** H**an**del

I have added the 'm' to help show that his birth country is mostly there in his name.

Another easy fact to remember is that he wrote music for King George I and King George II. Seeing as his own name was George, that should be fairly easy to remember.

Gustav Holst

Famous for his work *The Planets*, we need to find a way to associate his name with something that will remind us of planets.

Look at his first and second names. Is there anything similar in them. Yes, there is... the letters 'st' appear in both, beside each other, Gu**st**av Hol**st**, and they are the only letters to appear twice. So that is our anchor - 'st' – because it **st**ands out. So, planets and 'st'...

What do planets orbit around?

A **st**ar! So you know the clue to what Gustav Holst

wrote is in his name if he comes up as a question in your test.

Sir Edward Elgar

Questions regarding the *Last Night of the Proms* at the Royal Albert Hall seem to come up fairly regularly, so it's a good idea to be aware of the fact the Edward Elgar wrote *The Pomp and Circumstances Marches (Land of Hope and Glory)*. Unfortunately there aren't many visual prompts from his name to associate with this. Probably the best way is to think of (Eng)-land of Hope and Glory and use the association with the 'E', 'l', 'g' and 'a' from Elgar to trigger the England connection. Not ideal, but your brain will group this in with the rest of your composer anchors and ought to be able to make the association if a question on this comes up in your test.

Ralph Vaughan Williams

Not a lot is said in *A modern, thriving society* about Ralph Vaughan Williams other than he was influenced by folk music. Perhaps not much to go on, but let's have a think... Ralph Vaughan Williams... RVW... Sounds like 'Our VW.'

Volkswagen (VW) vans are sometimes associated with hippy people, who are hugely into folk music. If we imagine 'our VW' van (RVW) painted in psychedelic colours and with folk music being played from it, we have a very strong visual image to associate Ralph Vaughan Williams with folk music.

Sir William Walton

Again, not a lot is said in *A modern, thriving society* about William Walton, except we already know that he was one of our unfortunate composers caught in the giant spider web. Think of the fact that he might end up being a feast for the giant spider and you will be able to associate him with his work *Balthazar's Feast*. (As his name is the 'w' in web, this should prevent you confusing Elgar or Britten with the feast, for whom you will have different images for their individual associations.)

Benjamin Britten

Benjamin Britten founded the Aldeburgh festival in Suffolk, which *A modern, thriving society* says is of 'international importance'. If we think of Britain as being made up of various countries, we can associate Britain/Britten with the word 'international'. Once again, a massive clue in the name. Also, remember that one of Britten's works is called *Billy Budd*. He has the same initials!

So that's composers covered. There are some really good visual images there which will definitely help you to make associations with all seven of them.

How would you answer this question?

The composer George Frederick Handel (1695-1759) was born in _____ and spent many years in the UK and became a British citizen in 1727

○ Iceland

○ Germany

○ Japan

○ Russia

And how about this one?

The following are TWO famous UK sportsmen and women: (Choose any 2 answers)

- Benjamin Britten
- Steve Redgrave
- Henry Purcell
- Mo Farah

That was arguably a tricky one as the question was about sportspeople, not composers. The lesson if you ticked the two composers we were just taking about and got it wrong – make sure you read the question and not what you think the question is! The test is 45 minutes long so there is absolutely no need to rush it. Rushing might lead to mistakes so practice being slow, calm and steady.

You can use the same approach as we used for composers for the ten 'Notable British Artists' also covered in *A modern, thriving society* and the nine 'Notable Authors and Writers'. Try and use images which are personal to you – maybe ones based on your own favourite art work or books that you have read. Follow the same approach as we did for the composers and you will find that your brain automatically categorises each field separately.

Leisure

Another thing worth knowing is the national flowers associated with each of the countries in the UK. They are as follows:

Wales – the daffodil

England – the rose

Northern Ireland – the shamrock

Scotland – the thistle

I have placed them in that order above for a very specific purpose – the flower names are in alphabetical order – d, r, s, and t. Let's take a look at the UK map again and see how we can remember all of the national flowers using just one symbol. I have put the first letter of the national flower in the respective country.

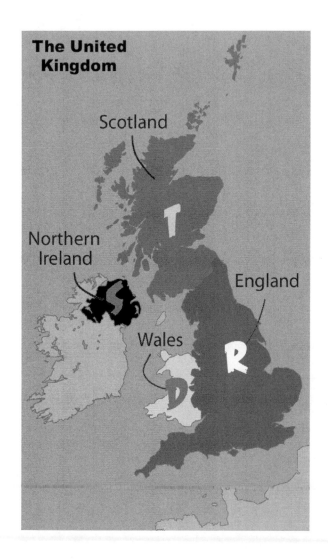

You'll see a very noticeable direction of travel from the left to the right, then all the way over to the left and then right again. You can plot the points by the extremities of the symbol, which looks like a large letter 'S'.

By simply remembering that 'S' shape with the arrow at the top showing you the direction, all you need to know about the national flowers is there. Progress alphabetically and you will start with 'd'. You know that Wales is the first country because it is bottom left, therefore Wales equals 'd' equals daffodil. You know the direction of travel as the 'S' bends out to the right. That's England, and the next flower must begin with 'r' because the order is alphabetical, therefore England equals rose, and so on.

Just remember:

F L O W E R  !

England has _____ flower associated with it and sometimes worn on national saints' day

◉ the rose

◉ the thistle

◉ the daffodil

◉ the shamrock

This question is perfect because it names all of the flowers and you can then put them into alphabetical order and plot them on the map according to the symbol. You know that England comes second in the 's' so once you have put the flowers into alphabetical order, it must be the second flower.

Places of interest

Probably the easiest section of the entire learning material as most of these are asking you to name landmarks. There is probably no need to say that the London Eye looks like an eye because it is round, and that Edinburgh Castle looks like a castle... Sometimes mnemonics are simply not required and it is better to just learn these by looking at the pictures in the *Life in the United Kingdom – A Guide For New Residents.*

Now we've done a few mnemonic exercises based on *A modern, thriving society*, it's time for some more questions. First of all, let's take a trip down memory lane and try the same ten questions you answered earlier, before you started using mnemonics, just to see if you feel you have retained what you have been learning.

LIFE IN THE UK – Passing your Life In The UK test

Question 1 of 10

1. When is Boxing Day?

- The day after Christmas Day
- The day before Christmas Day
- 31 December
- 1 January

Question 2 of 10

2. Who is a Scottish Cyclist who has won six Gold Olympic medals?

- Sir Chris Hoy
- Sir Ian Botham
- Dame Ellen MacArthur
- David Weir

Question 3 of 10

3. When is Valentine's Day?

- 15 February
- 14 February
- 16 February
- 12 February

Question 4 of 10

4. The main Olympic site for the 2012 Olympic games was in

- Oxford Street, West London
- Stratford, East London
- Millenium Stadium in Cardiff
- Wembley Stadium in London

Question 5 of 10

5. Is the statement below TRUE or FALSE? Snowdonia is a national park in North Wales.

- FALSE
- TRUE

106

6. Which two are Protestant Christian groups in the UK?

- [ ] Buddhists
- [ ] Roman Catholics
- [ ] Methodists
- [ ] Baptists

7. Who won the men's singles in the US open in 2012?

- ( ) David Weir
- ( ) Andy Murray
- ( ) Jessica Ennis
- ( ) Ellie Simmonds

8. Diwali normally falls in

- ( ) October or November
- ( ) January or Februaury
- ( ) August or September
- ( ) June or July

9. When is St Patrick's Day?

- ( ) 17 March
- ( ) 1 March
- ( ) 23 April
- ( ) 30 November

10. Which TWO of the following are famous horse-racing events?

- [ ] Royal Ascot
- [ ] The Grand National
- [ ] Grand Slam
- [ ] Champions League

How did it feel this time? Better than before? We covered a few of them so you should have found that some of them triggered your mnemonics.

Let's try another ten. There's no time limit – relax and take as long as you need. The important thing you need to do here is to use the mnemonics whenever you see something we have covered. I know it might at first feel like a jumble of strange maps of the UK and people spilling stew onto their lovely white trousers, but remember the stories behind the images and the links they will lead to...

Mini Test 2 – 10 Questions...

1. What is the name of the UK currency?

○ Rupee
○ Pound sterling
○ Taka
○ Euro

2. What is the capital city of the UK?

○ Washington DC
○ London
○ New York
○ Cardiff

3. Which of the following statement is correct?

○ The most famous competition is the Ashes, which is a series of Test matches played between England and Australia.
○ The most famous competition is the Ashes, which is a series of Test matches played between England and America.

4. Diwali normally falls in

○ June or July
○ October or November
○ August or September
○ January or Februaury

5. Which is the most famous tennis tournament hosted in Britain?

○ The Wimbledon Championships
○ The Premier League
○ The Ashes
○ The UEFA Champions League

6. Is the statement below TRUE or FALSE? Boxing Day is a public holiday.

- ○ FALSE
- ○ TRUE

7. Who is the patron saint of Wales?

- ○ St David
- ○ St Patrick
- ○ St George
- ○ St Andrew

8. Who won the Formula 1 world championship three times?

- ○ Bobby Moore
- ○ Sir Jackie Stewart
- ○ Dr Sir Ludwig Guttman
- ○ Christopher Dean

9. Which TWO facts are correct about Diwali?

- ☐ Diwali lasts for ten days.
- ☐ Diwali is often called the Festival of Lights.
- ☐ It is celebrated by Hindus and Sikhs.
- ☐ There is a famous celebration of Diwali in London.

10. Who is a Scottish Cyclist who has won six Gold Olympic medals?

- ○ Sir Ian Botham
- ○ Dame Ellen MacArthur
- ○ Sir Chris Hoy
- ○ David Weir

How were they? Not too bad, I hope! The answers to both mini-tests are right at the very end of this book. Were there a few answers you got right with the help of some of your new learning techniques? If so, congratulations! You are well on your way! Hopefully you remembered the following, all of which have been discussed:

- Australia playing England in the Ashes (Q3)
- Needing a light in October/November for Diwali (Q4)
- David (Cameron) marching in Wales (Q7)
- Jackie Stewart driving you around fast in his car, making you spill your stew (Q8)
- A circus (Sir Chris) clown on a bicycle (Q10)

It is at this stage that (hopefully) you will agree that as bizarre, silly and surreal some of the things we have looked at are, there is no denying that they *do* stick in your mind and they *do* allow you to recall a much larger amount of information than just reading facts. Even if you had found yourself getting irritated by all of the images and scenarios, maybe now you are starting to appreciate how helpful they can be. Take the David Cameron mnemonic, for example, when he was marching in the puddle in Wales. Can you also recall who else was with him on the UK map and where they were stood? And what they were doing? You almost certainly can, I'm sure.

I remember the absolute buzz of excitement I got when I first realised that this technique actually worked for me. It instantly transformed my most-difficult modules into my new favourites as I set about making images and mind-maps to break the information down into things I could understand and piece together into something that made sense. I hope you're starting to feel that too.

CHAPTER 6

PEOPLE POWER

TEN MORE CHARACTER PROFILES

I've put together ten mini-profiles on some of the people referred to in *Life in the United Kingdom – A Guide For New Residents* to help you remember them as people and not just facts. Before you sit your test, compose some of your own. The glossary at the end of the *Life in the United Kingdom – A Guide For New Residents* book is a good place to pick some out from. They are quick to do and the research into them is a great way to engage your brain. Plus, the quirky things you might find out may prove to be the difference between getting an answer wrong or right.

We will look at the types of questions you might be asked on some of them too.

1. King Richard III

King Richard III of the House of York was killed in the Battle of Bosworth Field in

- ○ 1485
- ○ 1490
- ○ 1495
- ○ 1498

We can remember that King Richard III died in 1485 because 'died' and '5' rhyme. As a visual, something silly like a massive '85' falling out of the sky and heading straight for King Richard III might also work.

Richard III was a colourful character. He was often depicted as having a hunched back, although this may have been exaggerated by the people who weren't very fond of him and who wrote the history books. He was also suspected of making his two nephews 'disappear' so that he would be next in line for the throne.

2. Anne Boleyn

Anne Boleyn the wife of Henry VIII was a _____ princess, she and Henry had one daughter, Elizabeth

- German
- French
- English
- Spanish

Anne Boleyn the wife of Henry VIII was accused of taking lovers so she was executed at

- Pendennis Castle
- Peckforton Castle
- Red Lion Tower
- The Tower of London

A very sad story, is Anne's. She was an English princess and the second wife of Henry VIII. She was executed at The Tower of London after being accused of all sorts, including incest and treason.

The accusations are generally accepted to have been entirely false and Anne is remembered for her calm composure on the day of her execution.

3. William Shakespeare

Some of the famous lines from William Shakespeare's plays and poems which are still often quoted are:
(Choose any 2 answers)

☐ By all the means you can

☐ A rose by any other name

☐ Listen to many, speak to a few

☐ All the world's a stage

Shakespeare is renowned as the English playwright

○ True

○ False

William Shakespeare is famous for writing:
(Choose any 2 answers)

☐ TV dramas

☐ Poems

☐ Plays

☐ Newspaper articles

So amazing was William Shakespeare that some people don't believe that he could have possibly written everything he is credited with writing.

He was a prolific playwright, poet and actor, but very little is actually known about him as a person, leading to many theories about his life.

4. Clement Attlee

Who was the new Prime Minister in 1945?

○ Clement Attlee

○ Dylan Thomas

○ Ernest Rutherford

○ William Beveridge

Which political party did Clement Attlee, Prime Minister of the UK, belong to?

○ a) Tories
○ b) Labour
○ c) Liberal Democrats
○ d) Scottish National Party

Clement Attlee was a Labour politician who became Prime Minister in 1945 and remained so until 1951.

He was famous for smoking a pipe. In public he was seen as modest and unassuming. His strengths emerged behind the scenes, especially in committees where his depth of knowledge, quiet demeanour and pragmatism proved decisive.

To use his name as an anchor, image the word 'Battle'. At the 'end' of the 'Battle' is '-attle', which is pretty close to Attlee. So if you remember that the Second World War (Battle) ended in 1945, you have an anchor for when Clement Attlee became Prime Minister... end of the battle equals Attlee.

5. Jane Austen

Jane Austen and Charles Dickens both are famous

○ painters

○ novelists

○ worriers

The name of a novel by Jane Austen is _____

○ Our Man in Havana

○ Sense and Sensibility

○ Oliver Twist

○ Far from the Madding Crowd

Which of these people are famous UK sports stars? (Choose any 2 answers)

☐ Sir Chris Hoy

☐ Jane Austen

☐ Lucien Freud

☐ Dame Kelly Holmes

Jane Austen was a nineteenth century English novelist. Two of her famous novels are *Sense and Sensibility* and *Pride and Prejudice*.

There appear to be lots of questions about her on the test, so she is definitely worth remembering in case she pops up on yours. To help you, here's an amusing fact: *Sense and Sensibility* and *Pride and Prejudice* were both re-written in recent years and renamed *Sense and Sensibility and Sea Monsters* and *Pride and Prejudice and Zombies*.

6. Gordon Brown

A member of the Labour Party, Gordon Brown is Scottish and was the Prime Minister of Britain from 2007 to 2010.

Interesting fact: He is blind in his left eye.

7. Bloody Mary

King Henry VIII's daughter Mary was a devout Catholic and persecuted Protestants, which is why she became known as

- Catholic Mary
- Scary Mary
- Bloody Mary
- Killer Mary

The Catholic Queen, known as 'Bloody Mary', was the daughter of Henry VIII and which of his six wives?

- a) Jane Seymour
- b) Catherine Howard
- c) Catherine of Aragon
- d) Elizabeth I

Bloody Mary was the daughter of Henry VIII and his first wife, Catherine of Aragon.

She was a Catholic monarch and got her rather unpleasant nickname as a result of her treatment of Protestants.

8. Winston Churchill

In 2002, a public vote decided that Winston Churchill was the Greatest Briton of all time

⦿ True

⦿ False

During the _____ World War Winston Churchill was the British Prime Minister

⦿ First

⦿ Second

Winston Churchill was voted the Greatest Briton of all time in 2002 and he was the British Prime Minister during the Second World War (he also fought in the First World War).

Churchill was famous for his electrifying speeches. He was a member of the Conservative Party.

It may help you to remember the image of a *church* on top of a *hill*, with lots of soldiers around it, to connect him to the Second World War.

9. Sir Francis Drake

Which of these are associated with Sir Francis Drake? (Choose any 2 answers)

☐ Sailing around the world

☐ The Titanic

☐ The Spanish Armada

☐ Empress of Ireland

Sir Francis Drake's ship the 'Golden Hind', was one of the first to sail right around/circumnavigate _____

○ the Ireland

○ the United Kingdom

○ the Europe

○ the world

English Admiral Sir Francis Drake circumnavigated the globe in 1577-78, helped defeat the Spanish Armada and was the most renowned seaman of the Elizabethan era.

Before he began his round the world trip, Drake was involved in piracy and the illicit slave trade.

With his surname, you can imagine a duck in water, as a drake is a male duck. Imagine the duck swimming around the world and it will trigger what you know of Sir Francis Drake. If it also helps, imagine the duck has a golden tail to remind you of *The Golden Hind*.

10. Florence Nightingale

Which of these were famous Victorians? (Choose any 2 answers)

☐ Dylan Thomas

☐ Florence Nightingale

☐ Isambard Kingdom Brunei

☐ Margaret Thatcher

Florence Nightingale is famous for her work on children's education in the 19th century

○ True

○ False

Florence Nightingale was a Victorian and was the founder of modern nursing. She came to prominence during the Crimean War, where she organised the treatment of wounded soldiers and earned the nickname 'The Lady with the Lamp', as she would make rounds to attend to the soldiers during the night.

131

Our anchor here will be the word 'Night' in Florence's surname. It's nice and easy – it's night time so she needs a lamp to see where she is going.

These profiles are quick and easy to do and it is really helpful to have an image for each one, particularly if it is a cartoon, as they tend to be exaggerated and therefore easier to remember and recall. As suggested, you can go through the glossary of *Life in the United Kingdom – A Guide For New Residents* and select names from there. I really recommend this approach. Taking three or four minutes to prepare a profile will help you to remember the person so much more than just reading about them from the *Guide*.

CHAPTER 7

A FINAL WORD

Now that we've reached the end of the book (from here on, it's practice questions and answers), time for another, fuller apology to finish off the one which started the books. At times, you may have noticed that I have appeared quite cynical and irreverent towards a variety of topics and people mentioned in this book. For what it's worth, many of them do not in fact reflect my true opinions. For example, I thought the London 2012 Olympic Games were great and I even went to watch some of the athletics enjoyed the fantastic atmosphere. Referring to it somewhat harshly was intended to highlight the absurdity of naming so many 2012 athletes as seemingly *essential* to know about in order to demonstrate "sufficient knowledge of British life". It reveals more about the time the learning material for the test was put together than it does about British life, so making you aware of this was another way to get you to tame the beast.

For most of the cynicism, believe me, I had your best interests at heart – I wanted to say things which stuck in your memory and maybe even got a bit of a reaction from you.

Trust me, you'll find that you remember things a lot more clearly if there is even a little bit of emotion involved! To fans of Andy Murray, I apologise the most. I'm certain he's a smashing guy. But to those of you who had never heard of him, look at his name now... Andy... Murray... Andy... Murray... on and on. At least now you have more of a mental jog as to who he is and what he has achieved.

To cricket fans... well, I really do not like cricket. That part was true. But my reference to the Ashes hopefully helped you if you don't know much about cricket when the question came up in one of the practice tests.

Before I let you make a start on the ten practice tests which follow, I wish you all the very best in your actual test and hope that having read this book you will approach it with enthusiasm and confidence. I also wish you all the best beyond the successful completion of your test and hope that passing it helps you to achieve all that you want. Enjoy your life in the UK!

Finally, I'd be delighted to hear from you in the review sections of Amazon and iTunes if you can spare the time. Let me know what you might have enjoyed about this book or what you think might work better for future editions.

And of course, please do let me know how you get on with the test... I'm sure you'll do great.

The very best of luck to you!

TEN FULL PRACTICE TESTS

The following tests cover the entire *Life in the United Kingdom – A Guide For New Residents*, not just the section we have focussed on in Chapter 5. They are therefore designed to be taken after you have applied your new learning method to the other chapters in the official guide.

The answers are at the end of each individual test.

Practice test one

1.   _____ **is a fundamental principle of British life**

   ○ The rule of law

   ○ The rule of the upper classes

   ○ The rule of your local member of Parliament (MP)

   ○ The rule of the monarch

2.   **Who established the Church of England?**

   ○ Henry VII

   ○ Edward VI

   ○ Henry VIII

   ○ King Richard III

3.   **Courts deal with minor criminal cases in the UK are: (Choose any 2 answers)**

   ☐ Crown Court

   ☐ Justice of the Peace Court

   ☐ Centre Court

   ☐ Coroner's Court

   ☐ Magistrates' Court

4. **If a judge finds that a public body is not respecting someone's legal rights, they can (Choose any 2 answers)**

☐ order them to change their practices

☐ place its members in prison

☐ close down the public body

☐ order them to pay compensation

5. **The Prime Minister can be changed if (Choose any 3 answers)**

☐ the queen orders

☐ the MPs in the governing party decide to do so

☐ he or she wishes to resign

☐ the House of Commons decide to do so

☐ his or her party loses a General Election

☐ he or she do not answer the phone for 2 days

6. **_____ developed horse-driven spinning mills that used only one machine**

○ Richard Arkwright

○ Adam Smith

○ James Watt

○ Howard Florey

7. **_____ is the process of preparing fibres for spinning into yarn and fabric**

○ Cordmill

○ Spindering

○ Milling

○ Carding

8. **The first man to be called the Prime Minister was _____, who was Prime Minister from 1721 to 1742**

○ Isaac Newton

○ Sir Robert Walpole

○ Ernest Rutherford

○ Howard Florey

9. **The East India Company, originally set up to trade, gained control of large parts of India**

○ True

○ False

10. **London's West End, also known as _____, is a particularly well known theatre district**

○ Theatreworld

○ Theatreland

○ Theatreboom

○ Westtheatre

11. **When did the English defeat the Spanish Armada, which had been sent by Spain to conquer England and restore Catholicism?**

○ 1455

○ 1488

○ 1544

○ 1588

12. **One of the most important principles of the Enlightenment was that**

○ everyone should have the right to their own political and religious beliefs

○ newspapers should be free from political involvement

○ everyone should have the right to the vote

13. **All young people in the UK are sent a National Insurance number just before their**

○ 13th birthday

○ 14th birthday

○ 16th birthday

○ 18th birthday

14. **_____ was the first to be extensively covered by media**

○ The First World War

○ The Second World War

142

○ The Boer War

○ The Crimean War

15. **Civil war between the king and Parliament began in _____**

○ 1622

○ 1632

○ 1642

○ 1652

16. **_____ defeated a Scottish army in the Battles of Dunbar and Worcester**

○ Robert Burns

○ Oliver Cromwell

○ William Shakespeare

○ Isaac Newton

17. **In November 2012, the public elected Police and Crime Commissioners (PCCs) in (Choose any 2 answers)**

☐ England

☐ Wales

☐ Scotland

☐ Northern Ireland

18. **The Scots had _____ to the execution of Charles I and declared his son Charles II to be king**

○ agreed

○ not agreed

19. **Commonwealth members are (Choose any 4 answers)**

☐ Bangladesh

☐ Czech Republic

☐ Germany

☐ India

☐ Poland

☐ South Africa

☐ Spain

☐ UK

20. **Some constituencies were controlled by a single wealthy family, but other constituencies had hardly any voters and were called _____**

○ county boroughs

○ rotten boroughs

○ Parliamentary boroughs

○ pocket boroughs

21. **There are _____ members of the Scottish Parliament (MSPs)**

○ 109

○ 119

○ 129

○ 139

22. **During the First World War _____ and _____ countries/empires were part of the Central Powers (Choose any 2 answers)**

☐ Belgium

☐ Bulgaria

☐ Italy

☐ The Austro-Hungarian Empire

23. **On the official flag of the UK, what does the cross of St George represent?**

○ England

○ Scotland

○ Wales

○ Ireland

24. **Night clubs with dancing and music usually open and close _____ than pubs**

○ earlier

○ later

Answers to practice test one

1 The rule of law, 2 Henry VIII, 3 Justice of the Peace Court & Magistrates' Court

4 Order them to change their practices and order them to pay compensation

5 The MPs in the governing party decide to do so, He or she wishes to resign, His or her party loses a General Election, 6 Richard Arkwright, 7 Carding, 8 Sir Robert Walpole, 9 True, 10 Theatreland,

11 1588, 12 Everyone should have the right to their own political and religious beliefs

13 16th birthday, 14 The Crimean War, 15 1642, 16 Oliver Cromwell, 17 England and Wales, 18 Not agreed, 19 Bangladesh, India, South Africa and UK, 20 Rotten boroughs, 21 129, 22 Bulgaria and Austro-Hungarian Empire, 23 England, 24 Later

Practice test two

1.   **The Roman Catholics in _____ were afraid of the growing power of the Puritans**

   ○ England

   ○ Scotland

   ○ Wales

   ○ Ireland

2.   **Who was recognised as the leader of the new republic?**

   ○ Robert Burns

   ○ Isaac Newton

   ○ Oliver Cromwell

   ○ William Shakespeare

3.   **During the 18th century, new ideas about politics, philosophy and science were developed, this is often called**

   ○ The Bard

   ○ Glorious Revolution

   ○ Hogmanay

   ○ The Enlightenment

4.   **In the 18th and 19th centuries the development of the Bessemer process for the mass production of steel led to the development of**
   (Choose any 2 answers)

   ☐ hospitals

☐ the shipbuilding industry

☐ motorways

☐ the railways

5. **An aim of the United Nations is**

○ to examine decisions made by the European Union

○ to create a single free trade market

○ to promote dictatorship

○ to prevent war and promote international peace and security

6. **When is the Boxing day?**

○ 24th December

○ 25th December

○ 26th December

○ 27th December

7. **Britain was the first country to industrialise on a large scale**

○ True

○ False

8. **Oliver Cromwell was _____ of the English republic**

○ the King

○ the leader

○ the artist

○ the clans

9.   **The Brit Awards is an event where _____ are given awards**

○ sports people

○ rich people

○ musicians

○ poor people

10.   **During the Industrial Revolution in the 18th and 19th centuries children also worked in the factories and were treated in the same way as adults**

○ Yes, this is correct

○ No, children were not allowed to enter in the factories

11.   **Members of the House of Lords are**

○ not elected by the people

○ voted in by members of the House of Commons

○ elected by the general public

12.   **In 1314, which Scottish king defeated the English at the Battle of Bannockburn?**

○ Malcolm

○ William Wallace

○ Andrew

○ Robert the Bruce

13. **For a legal advice you can contact:
(Choose any 2 answers)**

☐ The Citizens Advice Bureau

☐ Your local member of Parliament (MP)

☐ A local councillor

☐ A solicitor

14. **The event was called the 'Glorious Revolution'
because there was no fighting in _____**

○ England

○ Scotland

○ Wales

○ Ireland

15. **UK landmarks are:
(Choose any 2 answers)**

☐ Edinburgh Castle

☐ The Eisteddfod

☐ The London Eye

☐ National Trust

16. **Northern Ireland Assembly at**

○ Stormont, in Belfast

○ Lisburn, in Belfast

○ Newtownabbey, in Belfast

○ Bangor, in County Down

17. **Adults who are eligible to vote in all UK elections includes:**
(Choose any 2 answers)

☐ Citizens of the Commonwealth who are resident in the UK

☐ Only those born in the UK

☐ UK-born and naturalised adult citizens

☐ Citizens of the other parts of Europe

18. **Which changes were introduced by the Education Act of 1944?**
(Choose any 2 answers)

☐ Free secondary education for all

☐ New public examinations for primary education

☐ Primary education for all

☐ A clear division between primary and secondary education

19. **National parks are**

○ areas of protected countryside that everyone can visit

○ national sports grounds for people to hold sporting events

20. **Political parties that formed the coalition government in 2010 are:**
    (Choose any 2 answers)

    ☐ Liberal Democrats

    ☐ Conservatives

    ☐ Labour

    ☐ Communists

21. **Life peers in the House of Lords are appointed by**
    _____

    ○ The monarch

    ○ The Prime Minister

    ○ The Speaker of the House of Commons

    ○ Members of Parliament (MPs)

22. **Famous UK landmarks are:**
    (Choose any 2 answers)

    ☐ Loch Lomond

    ☐ Snowdonia

    ☐ Notre Dame

    ☐ Grand Canyon

23. **A jury is made up of members of the _____ chosen at random from the local electoral register**

    ○ Parliament

    ○ public

○ local council

○ judges

24. **When is New Year's Day?**

○ 31st December

○ 1st January

○ 7th January

○ 1st February

Answers to practice test two

1 Ireland, 2 Oliver Cromwell, 3 The Enlightenment, 4 The Shipbuilding industry and the railways, 5 To prevent war and promote international peace and security, 6 26th December, 7 True, 8 The Leader,

9 Musicians, 10 Yes, this is correct, 11 Not elected by the people, 12 Robert the Bruce, 13 The Citizens Advice Bureau and a solicitor, 14 England, 15 Edinburgh Castle and The London Eye,

16 Stormont, in Belfast, 17 Citizens of the Commonwealth who are resident in the UK and UK-born and naturalised adult citizens, 18 Free secondary education for all and a clear division between primary and secondary education, 19 Areas of protected countryside that everyone can visit,

20 Liberal Democrats and Conservatives, 21 The monarch, 22 Loch Lomond and Snowdonia, 23 Public, 24 1st January

Practice test 3

1. **Example of civil law is**

   ○ Drunk and disorderly behaviour

   ○ Debt

   ○ Burglary

   ○ Violent crime

2. **The UK had high levels of employment during the Great Depression of the 1930s**

   ○ True

   ○ False

3. **The Chancellor of the Exchequer is responsible for the _____**

   ○ immigration

   ○ economy

   ○ crime

   ○ policing

4. **Henry VIII established the Church of England**

   ○ in order to start a war with the French

   ○ because the Pope refused to grant him a divorce

5. **A traditional pub game in the UK is**

   ○ Bowling

○ Rounders

○ Pool

○ Poker

6. **In 1979 Margaret Thatcher became famous in UK history because she**

○ campaigned to give women the voting rights same age as men

○ took part in the Falklands War

○ became the first woman Prime Minister

○ became a High Court judge

7. **Influential British bands are: (Choose any 2 answers)**

☐ The Royal Family

☐ The Rolling Stones

☐ The National Trust

☐ The Beatles

8. **The Highland Clearances occurred in**

○ England

○ Scotland

○ Northern Ireland

○ Wales

9. **A General Election occurs every six years**

○ True

○ False

10. **A bank holiday is**

○ a holiday just for people working in banks

○ a public holiday when banks and other businesses close for the day

○ a holiday entitlement for working longer hours than usual (overtime)

○ the day when all banks close to calculate the notes

11. **In Northern Ireland a member of your family must complete a voting registration form on your behalf**

○ True

○ False

12. **The National Trust is a**

○ charity that works for the homeless

○ charity that works to preserve important buildings in the UK

○ government-run organisation that provides funding for charities

○ charity for medical research

13. **As a citizen or permanent resident of the UK your responsibility will be to**

○ find illegal immigrants

158

○ keep your dog on a lead at all the time

○ look after yourself and your family

○ grow your own vegetables

14. **William Shakespeare is famous for writing:**
    (Choose any 2 answers)

    ☐ TV dramas

    ☐ Poems

    ☐ Plays

    ☐ Newspaper articles

15. **Famous British authors includes:**
    (Choose any 2 answers)

    ☐ Gustav Holst

    ☐ Thomas Hardy

    ☐ Mary Quant

    ☐ Henry Moore

    ☐ Graham Greene

16. **In 1066, _____ invaded England and**
    defeated King Harold at the Battle of Hastings

    ○ Canute

    ○ Harold of Wessex

    ○ Richard the Lionheart

    ○ William of Normandy

159

17. **The House of Lords mostly acts as the government wishes**

○ True

○ False

18. **When a member of Parliament (MP) dies or resigns**

○ the post remains vacant until the next General Election

○ a by-election is held to replace the member of Parliament

○ another MP looks after the constituency

○ their party chooses someone to fill the post until the next General Election

19. **Norwich, Plymouth and Leeds are cities in**

○ Scotland

○ Northern Ireland

○ England

○ Wales

20. **Jensen Button, Lewis Hamilton and Damon Hill are all British winners of the _____ Championship**

○ Athletics

○ Formula 1

○ Football

○ Skiing

21. **The minimum legal age to buy alcohol in the UK is**
_____

- ○ 16
- ○ 18
- ○ 19
- ○ 20

22. **The Wimbledon Championships are associated with soccer**

- ○ True
- ○ False

23. **In 1776, _____ colonies of the British Empire decided to declare their independence**

- ○ American
- ○ Australian
- ○ Canadian
- ○ South African

24. **The great thinkers of the Enlightenment were: (Choose any 2 answers)**

- ☐ Adam Smith
- ☐ Robert Louis
- ☐ Robert Burns

David Hume

Answers to practice test 3

1 Debt, 2 False, 3 Economy, 4 Because the Pope refused to grant him a divorce, 5 Pool, 6 Became the first woman Prime Minister, 7 The Rolling Stones and The Beatles, 8 Scotland, 9 False, 10 A public holiday when banks and other businesses close for the day, 11 False, 12 Charity that works to preserve important buildings in the UK, 13 Look after yourself and your family, 14 Poems and plays, 15 Thomas Hardy and Graham Greene, 16 William of Normandy, 17 False, 18 A by-election is held to replace the member of Parliament, 19 England, 20 Formula 1, 21 18, 22 False, 23 American, 24 Adam Smith and David Hume

Practice test 4

1. **Police forces are independent of the government**
   - ○ True
   - ○ False

2. **St Patrick's day is a public holiday in Northern Ireland**
   - ○ True
   - ○ False

3. **The members of the National Assembly for Welsh (AMs) can only speak in Welsh**
   - ○ Yes, this is correct
   - ○ No, they can also speak in English

4. **What is the capital city of Scotland?**
   - ○ Aberdeen
   - ○ Dundee
   - ○ Edinburgh
   - ○ Glasgow

5. **The jury has to listen to the evidence presented at the trial and then decide a verdict of 'guilty' or 'not guilty' based on what they have heard**

○ Yes, it's correct

○ No, they don't decide a verdict

6. **Remembrance Day November 11th commemorates those who died fighting for the UK and its allies**

○ True

○ False

7. **Anne of Cleves the wife of Henry VIII was a _____ princess**

○ German

○ French

○ Scottish

○ Spanish

8. **Guy Fawkes Night on 5th November goes back to 1605, when a small group of Catholics plotted to kill the Protestant King by using gunpowder to blow up the Houses of Parliament**

○ True

○ False

9. **Who is the head of state of the UK?**

○ Queen Elizabeth II

○ King George III

○ Queen Victoria

○ Winston Churchill

10. **There are a few MPs who do not represent any of the main political parties and they are called**

   ○ Self Member

   ○ Shadow Members

   ○ Oppositions

   ○ Independents

11. **The fundamental principles of British life include:**

   ○ Democracy

   ○ The rule of law

   ○ Individual liberty

   ○ Tolerance of those with different faiths and beliefs

   ○ Participation in community life

   ○ All of the above

12. **What is another name for the Church of England?**

   ○ The Catholic Church

   ○ The UK Church

   ○ The English

   ○ The Anglican Church

13. **You can buy alcohol in a shop or pub when you are 16 years old**

   ○ True

○ False

14. **People in the UK have to pay tax on their income, which includes:**
(Choose any 2 answers)

☐ Disability Living Allowance

☐ Profits from self-employment

☐ Income from property, savings and dividends

☐ Working/Child Tax Credit

☐ Child Benefit

☐ Maternity Allowance

15. **In each constituency, the candidate who gets the most votes is**

○ elected

○ collected

○ selected

16. **Judges can make decisions in disputes about contracts, property or employment rights or after an accident**

○ True

○ False

17. **To register to vote you have to _____**

○ Pay fees

○ Fill in a form

○ have to go to the MP

18. **British citizens can stand for office as a**

○ Member of Parliament

○ Local councillor

○ Member of the European Parliament

○ All of the above

19. **Britain has a constitutional Monarchy in which the King or The Queen have unlimited powers**

○ True

○ False

20. **A National Insurance number is**

○ a unique record for the NHS

○ a unique personal account number

○ a unique record for the Surgery

21. **In Scotland, the national Church is the Church of Scotland, which is a _____**

○ Protestant Church

○ Presbyterian Church

○ Methodists Church

○ Anglican Church

22. **In England, Wales and Northern Ireland, most minor criminal cases are dealt with in a**

   ○ Magistrates' Court

   ○ Justice of the Peace Court

23. **Who is the ceremonial head of the Commonwealth?**

   ○ The Foreign Secretary

   ○ The Queen

   ○ The Prime Minister

   ○ All of these

24. **Most towns and cities have a central shopping area, which is called _____**

   ○ the market

   ○ the town centre

   ○ the shopping club

   ○ car-boot sale

Answers to practice test 4

1 True, 2 True, 3 No, they can also speak in English, 4 Edinburgh, 5 Yes, it's correct, 6 True, 7 German, 8 True, 9 Queen Elizabeth II, 10 Independents, 11 All of the above, 12 The Anglican Church, 13 False, 14 Profits from self-employment and income from property, savings and dividends, 15 Elected, 16 True, 17 Fill in a form, 18 All of the above, 19 False, 20 A unique personal account number, 21 Presbyterian Church, 22 Magistrates' Court, 23 The Queen, 24 The town centre

Practice test 5

1. **The Northern Ireland Assembly has powers to decide on matters such as education, agriculture, environment, health, and social services**

   ○ True

   ○ False

2. **The National Trust was founded in _____ by three volunteers**

   ○ 1745

   ○ 1795

   ○ 1845

   ○ 1895

3. **Anne Boleyn the wife of Henry VIII was a _____ princess, she and Henry had one daughter, Elizabeth**

   ○ German

   ○ French

   ○ English

   ○ Spanish

4. **You will receive a fine of up to _____ if you watch TV but do not have a TV licence**

   ○ £200

   ○ £500

○ £800

○ £1,000

5. **What is the leader of the party that wins the election called?**

○ Shadow Ministers

○ Home Secretary

○ Chancellor of the Exchequer

○ Prime Minister

6. **When did hereditary peers lose the automatic right to attend the House of Lords?**

○ 1969

○ 1979

○ 1989

○ 1999

7. **You can buy alcohol if you are 17 years old**

○ True

○ False

8. **For most people, the right amount of income tax is automatically taken from _____ and paid directly to HM Revenue and Customs (HMRC)**

○ the income from employment by their employer

○ their bank account by direct debit

9. **The capital city of Wales is _____**

○ London

○ Belfast

○ Cardiff

○ Edinburgh

10. **Catherine of Aragon the wife of Henry VIII was a _____ princess**

○ German

○ French

○ English

○ Spanish

11. **People of the Iron Age sometimes defended sites called**

○ Hill forts

○ Hill barrows

○ Round barrows

○ Skara Brae

12. **Parts of the west of Britain, including much of what is now _____, remained free of Anglo-Saxon rule**
(Choose any 2 answers)

☐ England

☐ Scotland

☐ Northern Ireland

☐ Wales

13. **In England, parents and other community groups can apply to open a _____ school in their local area**

○ free

○ premium

○ affordable

14. **Stonehenge is in the English county of**

○ Berkshire

○ Hampshire

○ Wiltshire

○ Yorkshire

15. **Charities that work for the homeless are (Choose any 2 answers)**

☐ British Red Cross

☐ Age UK

☐ Crisis

☐ National Trust

☐ Shelter

16. **Who does not have to pay for a TV licence?**

○ People aged 60 or over

○ People aged 65 or over

○ People aged 70 or over

○ People aged 75 or over

17. **John Constable was**

  ○ An important contributor to the 'pop art' movement of the 1960s

  ○ A landscape painter, most famous for his works of Dedham Vale on the Suffolk-Essex border in the East of England

  ○ A very successful Northern Irish portrait painter

  ○ A Welsh artist, best known for his engravings and stained glass

18. **Who has an important ceremonial role in this country?**

  ○ The Queen

  ○ The Prime Minister

  ○ The Archbishop of Canterbury

19. **These ministers form the cabinet, a committee which usually meets _____ and makes important decisions about government policy**

  ○ daily

  ○ weekly

  ○ monthly

  ○ yearly

20. **If judges find that a public body is not respecting someone's legal rights, they can**

  ○ order that body to change its practices and/or pay compensation

174

○ ask the public body to come in the court and give the explanation

21. **You can find copies of Hansard report in large libraries and on the Internet**

○ True

○ False

22. **What percentage of people identified themselves as Sikh in the 2009 Citizenship Survey?**

○ 1%

○ 2%

○ 4%

○ 6%

23. **One TV licence covers all of the equipment at one address, but people who rent different rooms in a shared house must buy a separate TV licence**

○ True

○ False

24. **What sport is played at Wimbledon Championships?**

○ Rugby

○ Tennis

○ Football

○ Cricket

Answers to practice test 5

1 True, 2 1895, 3 English, 4 £1,000, 5 Prime Minister, 6 1999, 7 False, 8 The income from employment by their employer, 9 Cardiff, 10 Spanish, 11 Hill forts, 12 Scotland and Wales, 13 Free, 14 Wiltshire, 15 Crisis and Shelter, 16 People aged 75 or over, 17 A landscape painter, 18 The Queen, 19 Weekly, 20 Order that body to change its practices and/or pay compensation, 21 True, 22 1%, 23 True, 24 Tennis

Practice test 6

1. **The Prime Minister is**
    ○ in charge of the economy
    ○ The MP in charge of Health
    ○ The leader of the opposition party
    ○ The leader of the party in power

2. **The Norman Conquest was the last successful foreign invasion of _____ and led to many changes in government and social structures**
    ○ England
    ○ Scotland
    ○ Northern Ireland
    ○ Wales

3. **What do Seamus Heaney, Sir William Golding and Harold Pinter have in common?**
    ○ They have all been awarded the Nobel Prize for literature
    ○ They are all famous British singers
    ○ They were part of the first British expedition to the North Pole
    ○ They have all been Prime Minister

4. **No one has religious freedom in the UK**

○ True

○ False

5.   **What is the nickname for the great bell of the clock at the Houses of Parliament in London?**

○ London Eye

○ Snowdonia

○ The Eden Project

○ Big Ben

6.   **December 26th celebrates the birth of Jesus Christ**

○ True

○ False

7. **What type of government does the UK have?**

○ Dictatorship

○ Federal government

○ Parliamentary democracy

○ Communist government

8. **Does Britain have a written constitution?**

○ Yes

○ No

9. **Which of the following UK landmarks is in Northern Ireland?**

○ The Giant's Causeway

○ Stonehenge

○ The Eden Project

○ Snowdonia

10. **The Proms is _____ summer season of orchestral classical music**

○ a three-week

○ a four-week

○ a six-week

○ an eight-week

11. **During the _____ World War Winston Churchill was the British Prime Minister**

○ First

○ Second

12. **Civil servants**

○ have to be politically aligned to the elected government

○ are politically neutral

13. **The English fleet defeated a large French fleet of ships that Intended to land an army in England in 1588**

○ True

○ False

14. **Sir Steve Redgrave is a famous**

○ novelist

○ film actor who has won several BAFTAs

○ rower who won gold medals in five consecutive Olympic Games

15. **The last successful invasion of England was in**
_____

- ○ 1066
- ○ 1205
- ○ 1442
- ○ 1940

16. **Foods associated with England are: (Choose any 2 answers)**

- ☐ Haggis
- ☐ Fish and chips
- ☐ Roast beef
- ☐ Ulster fry

17. **Heroin, cocaine, ecstasy and cannabis are**

- ○ legal drugs
- ○ illegal drugs
- ○ medicine names

18. **The Roman army left Britain in AD _____ to defend other parts of the Roman Empire and never returned**

- ○ 110
- ○ 210
- ○ 310

○ 410

19. **Regarding the myth, when does Father Christmas come?**

    ○ Early in the morning

    ○ At midnight

    ○ At noon

20. **You can be fined or arrested if you consume alcohol in alcohol-free zones**

    ○ True

    ○ False

21. **In Ireland, the Black Death killed many in the Pale and, for a time, the area controlled by the English became larger**

    ○ Yes, this is correct

    ○ No, the area became smaller

22. **What is the national day of Northern Ireland?**

○ St George's

○ St Andrew's

○ St Patrick's

○ St David's

23. **The Chartists were campaigners who demanded the _____**

○ vote for women

○ vote for the working classes and other people without property

○ abolition of slavery

○ independence of Ireland

24. **The Commonwealth has no power over its members, although it can suspend membership**

○ True

○ False

Answers to practice test 6

1 The leader of the party in power, 2 England, 3 They have all been awarded the Nobel Prize for literature, 4 False, 5 Big Ben, 6 False, 7 Parliamentary democracy, 8 No, 9 The Giant's Causeway, 10 An eight-week, 11 Second, 12 Are politically neutral, 13 False, 14 Rower who won gold medals in five consecutive Olympic games, 15 1066, 16 Fish and chips, roast beef, 17 Illegal drugs, 18 410, 19 At midnight, 20 True, 21 No, the area became smaller, 22 St Patrick's, 23 Vote for the working classes and other people without property, 24 True

Practice test 7

1. **Traditionally, what do children do on Mother's Day?**

   ○ Take their mother for a Chinese meal

   ○ Take their mother to a park

   ○ Take their mother to the cinema

   ◉ Give gifts/cards to their mother

2. **Forced marriage is where one or both parties do not or cannot give their consent to enter into the partnership**

   ○ Yes, it's correct

   ○ No, it's incorrect

3. **The word 'Great Britain' refers to (Choose any 3 answers)**

   ☐ England

   ☐ Scotland

   ☐ Northern Ireland

   ☐ Wales

   ☐ Republic of Ireland

   ☐ Channel Islands

4. **When is Christmas Day?**

   ○ 1st January

○ 7th January

○ 23rd March

○ 25th December

5. **The Commonwealth Membership is**

○ compulsory

○ voluntary

6. **If you are arrested and taken to a police station, a police officer will tell you**

○ the reason for your arrest

○ to go back to home

○ to bring credit card or cheques

7. **How many countries are members of the Commonwealth?**

    ○ 36

    ○ 49

    ○ 54

    ○ 62

8. **The House of Lords has more powers then the House of Commons**

    ○ True

    ○ False

9. **What does MEP stand for?**

    ○ Member of the European Parliament

    ○ Minister of the European Parliament

    ○ Member of the Elected Parliament

    ○ Minister of the Elected Parliament

10. **People eat pancakes, which were traditionally made to use up foods such as egg, fat and milk before fasting during Lent**

    ○ True

    ○ False

11. **Solicitors are trained lawyers who give advice on legal matters, take action for their clients and represent their clients in court**

○ Yes, it's correct

○ No, solicitors cannot take action for their clients

12. **The Bronze Age was followed by _____**

○ the Stone Age

○ the Glass Age

○ the Iron Age

13. **Do you need to buy a TV Licence if there are no TVs in your house but you watch it on a computer/smart phone/tablet as it's being broadcast?**

○ Yes

○ No

14. **People open their Christmas presents during Easter**

○ True

○ False

15. **The government is usually formed by the party that wins the majority of constituencies**

○ True

○ False

16. **In England, Wales and Scotland, Magistrates and Justices of the Peace (JPs) usually work unpaid and do not need legal qualifications**

○ Yes, it's correct

○ No, they get paid

17. **The Queen can only, in a famous phrase,**

○ Rule, govern, and reign

○ Advise, warn and encourage

○ Revise, warn, and observe

○ Encourage, observe and advise

18. **Which one of these is England's largest national park?**

○ The Lake District

○ Snowdonia

○ Broads

○ Loch Lomond and the Trossachs

19. **During the period of 1600, Ireland was an almost completely _____ country**

○ Catholic

○ Irish

○ Protestant

20. **People in the UK are living longer than ever before because improved living standards and better health care**

○ True

○ False

21. **What is the Battle of Agincourt?**

○ The battle where the Scottish defeated the English

○ A decisive battle that allowed Romans to invade England

○ The most famous battle of the War of the Roses

○ The most famous battle of the Hundred Years War

22. **The Ceremonial duties performed by the monarch include, reading of Queen's Speech and opening and closing of Parliament**

   ○ True

   ○ False

23. **Police officers must (Choose any 3 answers)**

   ☐ themselves obey the law

   ☐ be rude or abusive

   ☐ not misuse their authority

   ☐ not make a false statement

   ☐ commit racial discrimination

24. **How many Assembly Members are there in the National Assembly for Wales?**

   ○ 50

   ○ 60

   ○ 75

   ○ 80

Answers to practice test 7

1 Give gifts/cards to their mother, 2 Yes, it's correct, 3 England, Scotland and Wales, 4 25th December, 5 Voluntary, 6 The reason for your arrest, 7 54, 8 False, 9 Member of the European Parliament, 10 True, 11 Yes, it's correct, 12 The Iron Age, 13 Yes, 14 False, 15 True, 16 Yes, it's correct, 17 Advise, warn and encourage, 18 The Lake District, 19 Catholic, 20 True, 21 The most famous battle of the Hundred Years War, 22 True, 23 Themselves obey the law, not misuse their authority, not make a false statement, 24 60

Practice test 8

1. **Employees**

   ○ do not have to pay for National Insurance contributions after the age of 60

   ○ have their National Insurance deducted from their pay by their employer

   ○ need to pay National Insurance Contributions

2. **Who is the head of state of the United Kingdom?**

   ○ The Foreign Secretary

   ○ The Prime Minister

   ○ The Queen

   ○ The MP

3. **When is Remembrance Day?**

   ○ November 5th

   ○ November 11th

   ○ November 25th

4. **The symbol of the House of Tudor was**

   ○ a red rose

   ○ a white rose

○ a red rose with a white rose inside it as a sign that the Houses of York and Lancaster were now allies

5. **School governors, or members of the school board in Scotland, are people from _____ who wish to make a positive contribution to children's education**

    ○ the school board

    ○ the local community

    ○ the teacher union

    ○ the Ministry of School

6. **Which official report is broadcast on digital TV?**

    ○ Parliamentary News

    ○ Hansard

    ○ None

7. **Money raised from income tax is being used for**
(Choose any 3 answers)

- ☐ Roads

- ☐ BBC TV and radio channels

- ☐ Education

- ☐ Water and drainage repair and maintenance

- ☐ State benefits

- ☐ Police and the armed forces

8. **The currency in the UK is the _____**

- ◯ euro

- ◯ pound sterling

- ◯ dollars

9. **In the 2009 Citizenship Survey, less than _____ of people identified themselves as Buddhist**

- ◯ 0.5%

- ◯ 1%

- ◯ 2%

- ◯ 4%

10. **A non-UK national living in the UK and looking for work, starting work or setting up as self-employed will need a**

○ Provisional Driving License

○ National Insurance number

○ Full Driving License

○ Birth Certificate

11. **What are the official reports of proceedings in Parliament known as?**

○ Hansards

○ White Papers

○ Green Papers

12. **Father's Day is the _____ Sunday in June**

○ first

○ second

○ third

○ forth

13. **Remembrance Day**

○ Keep alive the memory of Guy Fawkes

○ commemorates those who died fighting for the UK and its allies

○ Keeps alive the memory of those whose fought against the king

○ Celebrates the victory of world wars

14. **_____ had an important role in drafting the European Convention on Human Rights and Fundamental Freedoms**

○ British school teachers

○ British diplomats and lawyers

○ Chief Constables

○ The North Atlantic Treaty Organization (NATO)

15. **Northern Ireland Assembly has 120 members?**

○ True

○ False

16. **In eleventh hour, of the eleventh day, of the eleventh month in 1918 that the First World War (often called the Great War) was started**

○ War was started in 1911

○ Yes its right

○ No, it came to an end

17. **The queen of Scotland, much of Mary Stuart's childhood was spent in _____**

   ○ Germany

   ○ France

   ○ England

   ○ Scotland

18. **What documentation do you need to drive a motor vehicle?**

   ○ A driving licence and a mechanic's report on the engine

   ○ A road map and a receipt for the car/motorcycle

   ○ Driving licence, insurance, an MOT and road tax

   ○ A passport and a photo of your car/motorbike

19. **The Queen's residence in 10 Downing Street?**

   ○ True

   ○ False

20. **What is the function of the House of Lords?**

   ○   It give ex-MPs jobs

   ○   It has no function and should be declared illegal

   ○   It helps old judges keep an interest in things

   ○   It suggests amendments or proposes new laws

21. **The Council of Europe has power to make laws**

   ○   True

   ○   False

22. **There is a food that is traditionally associated with Northern Ireland is _____**

   ○   Roast beef, which is served with potatoes, vegetables, Yorkshire puddings

   ○   Fish and chips

   ○   Ulster fry - a fried meal with bacon, eggs, sausage, black pudding, white pudding, tomatoes mushrooms, soda bread and potato bread

   ○   Welsh cakes

   ○   Haggis - a sheep's stomach stuffed with offal, suet, onions and oatmeal

23. **In England, Wales and Northern Ireland, if an accused person is aged 10 to 17, the case is normally heard in a _____ in front of up to three specially trained magistrates or a District Judge**

    ○ Youth Court

    ○ Children's Court

    ○ Child Court

24. **There are 160 Members in The National Assembly for Wales**

    ○ True

    ○ False

Answers to practice test 8

1 Have their National Insurance deducted from their pay by their employer, 2 The Queen, 3 November 11th, 4 A red rose with a white rose inside it as a symbol that the Houses of York and Lancaster were now allies, 5 The local community, 6 Hansard, 7 Roads, education, police and the armed forces, 8 Pound, 9 0.5%, 10 National Insurance Number, 11 Hansards, 12 Third, 13 Commemorates those who died fighting for the UK and its allies, 14 British diplomats and lawyers, 15 False, 16 No, it came to an end, 17 France, 18 Driving license, insurance, an MoT and road tax, 19 False, 20 It suggests amendments or proposes new laws, 21 False, 22 Ulster fry, 23 Youth Court, 24 False

Practice test 9

1. **Around 4,000 years ago, people learned to make bronze, we call this period**
   - ○ the Stone Age
   - ○ the Bronze Age
   - ○ the Iron Age

2. **The Council of Europe is _____ for the protection and promotion of human rights in member countries**
   - ○ responsible
   - ○ not responsible

3. **St George is the Patron Saint of _____**
   - ○ Scotland
   - ○ Northern Ireland
   - ○ England
   - ○ Wales

4. **More serious civil cases (for example, when a large amount of compensation is being claimed) are dealt with in the _____ in England, Wales and Northern Ireland**
   - ○ Sheriff Court

   ○ County Court

   ○ High Court

   ○ Peace Courts

5.   _____ **first visited Britain in AD 789 to raid coastal towns and take away goods and slaves**

   ○ The Anglo-Saxons

   ○ The Norman Conquest

   ○ The Romans

   ○ The Vikings

6.   **In Scotland, serious cases are heard in a _____ with either a sheriff or a sheriff with a jury**

   ○ Crown Court

   ○ Magistrates' Court

   ○ Sheriff Court

7. **Good citizens are an asset to the UK**

   ○ True

   ○ False

8. **The Council of Europe has _____ member countries, including the UK**

   ○ 32

   ○ 37

   ○ 42

   ○ 47

9. **The UK is located in the _____ west of Europe**

   ○ east

   ○ south

   ○ north

   ○ centre

10. **There are also several islands which are closely linked with the UK but are not part of it: (Choose any 2 answers)**

    ☐ Northern Ireland

    ☐ The Channel Islands

    ☐ The Isle of Man

11. **In Britain its tradition to eat _____ on Christmas**

○ Lamb curry, Chicken Vindaloo, Milk pudding

○ Shepherd's pie, sausages and mash, chocolate cake

○ Roast turkey, Christmas pudding, Rich steamed pudding

○ Fish and chips

12. **The official name of the country is the United Kingdom of Great Britain and Northern Ireland**

○ True

○ False

13. **Cricket originated in _____ and is now played in many countries**

○ India

○ England

○ Australia

○ South Africa

14. **Areas of what is now Scotland were never conquered by**

  ○ The Ancient Greeks

  ○ The Romans

  ○ The Anglo-Saxons

  ○ The Vikings

15. **The United Kingdom's constitution is written by**

  ○ Parliament

  ○ The Archbishop of Canterbury

  ○ The Queen

  ○ It is an unwritten constitution

16. **Adult citizens of other EU states who are resident in the UK can vote in all elections**

  ○ True

  ○ False

17. **When did people learn how to make weapons and tools out of iron?**

  ○ In the Stone Age

  ○ In the Bronze Age

  ○ In the Iron Age

18. **In Elizabeth I's time, English settlers first began to colonise the eastern coast of**

○ America

○ Africa

○ China

○ Europe

19. **What are the Grand National, FA Cup, the 'Open' and Wimbledon?**

○ Sporting events

○ Shops in Knightsbridge

○ Famous places

○ Parks in London

20. **The second-largest party in the House of Commons is called**

○ the opposition

○ the cabinet

○ the country party

21. **The UK is a Security Council member of**
     _____

     ○ The European Parliament

     ○ The UK Parliament

     ○ The United Nation

22. **Eid ul-Fitr and Diwali are the National days**

     ○ Yes, it's right

     ○ No, these are European Cities

     ○ No, these are other religious days

23. **On April Fool's day people normally give each other presents**

     ○ True

     ○ False

24. **Many people continue to visit _____ for holidays and for leisure activities such as walking, camping and fishing**

     ○ shops

     ○ the countryside

     ○ banks

     ○ schools

Answers to practice test 9

1 The Bronze Age, 2 Responsible, 3 England, 4 High Court, 5 The Vikings, 6 Sheriff Court, 7 True, 8 47, 9 North, 10 The Channel Islands and the Isle of Man, 11 Roast turkey, Christmas pudding, Rich steamed pudding, 12 True, 13 England, 14 The Romans, 15 It is an unwritten constitution, 16 False, 17 In the Iron Age, 18 America, 19 Sporting events, 20 The opposition, 21 The United Nation, 22 No, these are other religious days, 23 False, 24 The countryside

Practice test 10

1. **Hadrian's Wall was built**

    ○ by the Piets (ancestors of the Scottish people) to keep out the Romans

    ○ on the orders of the Roman Emperor Hadrian

2. **EastEnders and Coronation Street are**

    ○ popular television programmes

    ○ historical landmarks

3. **How often does Prime Minister's Questions occur when Parliament is sitting?**

    ○ Every day

    ○ Once a week

    ○ Once a month

    ○ Twice a year

4. **For much of the Stone Age, Britain was connected to the continent by a**

    ○ Telephone line

    ○ Land bridge

    ○ Power line

5. **The Speaker of the House of Commons is**

○ Appointed by the Prime Minister

○ Heir to the throne

○ An ordinary MP

○ Appointed by the Queen

6. **The Queen is ceremonial head of**

○ The Commonwealth

○ The National Council for Voluntary Organisations (NCVO)

○ The North Atlantic Treaty Organization (NATO)

7. **_____ is the national flower of Wales**

○ The rose

○ The thistle

○ The daffodil

○ The shamrock

8. **As part of the citizenship ceremony, new citizens pledge to uphold its democratic values**

   ○ True

   ○ False

9. **A treaty gave independence to the south of Ireland in 1921**

   ○ True

   ○ False

10. **Members of the armed forces cannot stand for public office**

    ○ True

    ○ False

11. **The longest distance on the mainland is about _____ from John O'Groats on the north coast of Scotland to Land's End in the south-west corner of England**

    ○ 460 miles

    ○ 870 miles

    ○ 1540 miles

    ○ 2068 miles

12. **In the mid-17th century, the Civil War between Charles I and Parliament led to Oliver Cromwell becoming king of England**

    ○ True

○ False

13. **In the 1830s and 1840s a group called the Chartists campaigned for reform of the voting system**

○ True

○ False

14. **A jury is made up of**

○ People who are members of political parties

○ People randomly chosen from the electoral register

○ People who have submitted an application form and been accepted

○ People working in court under judge

15. **Benefits of volunteering are: (Choose any 2 answers)**

☐ Meeting new people

☐ Earning additional money

☐ Making your community a better place

☐ You are given a free bus pass to travel around the town

16. **During the 'Great Depression' of the 1930s, major new Industries developed were: (Choose any 2 answers)**

☐ Coal mining

☐ Aviation

☐ Shipbuilding

☐ Automobile

17. **You can serve on a jury up to the age of 75**

○ True

○ False

18. **Members of Parliament (MPs) are responsible for:**
(Choose any 2 answers)

☐ Supporting the government on all decisions and laws

☐ Scrutinising and commenting on what the government is doing

☐ Representing everyone in their constituency

☐ Representing only those who voted for them

19. **Who can only give 'advice, warn and encourage' about government matters?**

○ Prime Minister

○ Members of the public

○ The Queen

20. **_____ and his wife Jane Daly introduced 'shampooing', the Indian art of head massage, to Britain**

○ Richard Arkwright

○ Robert Burns

○ Sake Dean Mahomet

○ Isaac Newton

21. **The Chancellor of the Exchequer is responsible for the _____**

   ○ Legal affairs

   ○ Health

   ○ Education

   ○ Economy

22. **The National Citizen Service provides military training to young people**

   ○ True

   ○ False

23. **The Battle of Britain in 1940 was fought**

   ○ at the border

   ○ in the skies

   ○ at sea

24. **Once you are aged 17 or older, you can learn to drive**
   (Choose any 2 answers)

   ☐ Heavy goods vehicle

   ☐ Motor cycle

   ☐ Fire engine

   ☐ Car

Answers to practice test 10

1 On the orders of the Roman Emperor Hadrian, 2 Popular television programmes, 3 Once a week, 4 Land bridge, 5 An ordinary MP, 6 The Commonwealth, 7 The daffodil, 8 True, 9 True, 10 True, 11 870 miles, 12 False, 13 True, 14 People randomly chosen from the electoral register, 15 Meeting new people, making your community a better place, 16 Aviation and automobile, 17 False, 18 scrutinising and commenting on what the government is doing, representing everyone in their constituency, 19 The Queen, 20 Sake Dean Mahomet, 21 Economy, 22 False, 23 In the skies, 24 Motor cycle and car

A modern, thriving society - notes at a glance

- Population: 62 million people (2012)
- Population is ageing
- 70% Christian
- 4% Muslim
- 2% Hindu
- 1% Sikh
- 0.5% Jewish or Buddhist
- 21% no religion
- Church of England is Protestant
- Church of Scotland is Presbyterian
- St David's day (Wales): March 1
- St Patrick's day (N Ireland): March 17
- St George's day (England): April 23
- St Andrew's day (Scotland): November 30
- Only Scotland and N Ireland have holidays on saint's days
- Diwali, festival of lights, Sikhs, 5 days, usually oct or nov
- Hanukkah, Jewish, 8 days, nov or dec
- Eid al-Fitr, end of Ramadan, Muslim
- Eid ul Adha, Muslim
- Vaisakhi, Sikh, April 14
- Mother's Day, three weeks before Easter
- Father's day, third Sunday in June
- Cricket games can last for up to 5 goddamn days. Ashes.
- Football is most popular sport. Premier League, UEFA, Champions League, FIFA (one from each UK country), World Cup (same), UEFA (same)

- Rugby: 19th century England. Six Nations (union), Super League (league)
- Horse racing: Royal Ascot (Berkshire), Grand National (Liverpool), Scottish Grand National (Ayr)
- Golf: 15th C Scotland. Open Championship
- Tennis: England, 19th century. Leamington Spa, 1872. Wimbledon.
- Skiing: 5 centres in Scotland, world's longest dry slope near Edinburgh

Sports people

- Running: Roger Bannister, Mo Farah, Kelly Holmes
- Formula 1: Jackie Stewart, Damon Hill, Lewis Hamilton, Jensen Button
- Football: Bobby Moore
- Cricket: Ian Botham
- Ice dancing: Jayne Torvill and Christopher Dean
- Rowing: Steve Redgrave
- Paralympics: Tanni Grey-Thompson, David Weir, Ellie Simmonds
- Sailing: Ellen MacArthur (1976-), Francis Chichester (first solo circumnavigation)
- Cycling: Chris Hoy (1976-), Bradley Wiggins (1980-)
- Athletics: Jessica Ennis (1986-)
- Tennis: Andy Murray (1987-)

Music and art

- Purcell, Handel, Holst, Elgar, Vaughan Williams, Walton, Britten
- Festivals: Glastonbury, Isle of Wight, V Festival

Your notes

Your notes

Your notes

Your notes

Your notes

Your notes

Your notes

Your notes

Your notes

Your notes

Your notes

Answers to Mini-Test 1

The answers to the first ten practice questions from Chapter 5.

1. The day after Christmas Day
2. Sir Chris Hoy
3. 14 February
4. Stratford, East London
5. True
6. Methodists and Baptists
7. Andy Murray
8. October or November
9. 17 March
10. Royal Ascot and the Grand National

Answers to Mini-Test 2

The answers to the second ten practice questions from Chapter 5.

1. Pound
2. London
3. The most famous competition is the Ashes, which is a series of Test matches played between England and Australia

4. October or November

5. The Wimbledon Championships

6. True

7. St David

8. Sir Jackie Stewart

9. Diwali is often called Festival of Lights and it is celebrates by Hindus and Sikhs

10. Sir Chris Hoy

Made in the USA
Middletown, DE
22 September 2015